Thank you for returning
your books on time.

Abington Free Library
1030 Old York Road
Abington, PA 19001

GAYLORD

Tales and Traditions
of
Scottish Castles

Tales and Traditions
of
Scottish Castles

Nigel Tranter

BARNES
&NOBLE
BOOKS
NEW YORK

Contents

v

Foreword

All my life, even from school-days, I have been interested and excited by Scotland's magnificent heritage in castellated architecture, both in the sturdy and characterful buildings themselves and in their dramatic and colourful histories. Indeed, my first book, The *Fortalices and Early Mansions of Southern Scotland, 1400-1650*, was on this theme, before I ever started to write novels. And when I came to tackle the subject with rather more maturity and thoroughness, in the five volumes of The Fortified House in Scotland, in later life, it was the recognition of the vast and all but untapped wealth of story and tradition enshrined in the literally thousands of Scotland's castles, keeps and peel-towers — stories which never appear in academic history-books — which set me off on writing the long series of historical novels which looks like keeping me going until my dying day.

This book, then, is about just a few of those castles and their stories, 45 in fact, just selected brush strokes from a huge canvas, not necessarily the most notable or impor-tant, my more or less haphazard choice — save that I have sought to spread them well across the country, and have deliberately excluded some which are very well-known anyway, such as the Devil's card-game at Glamis, Montrose's apprehension at Ardvreck, the walled-up babe at Edinburgh Castle, and so on.

So the book is not about architecture but about people, families, incidents, mysteries, and only incidentally about history. But history has been called the memory of the race — and it would be a pity indeed if some of these memories were lost.

Nigel Tranter

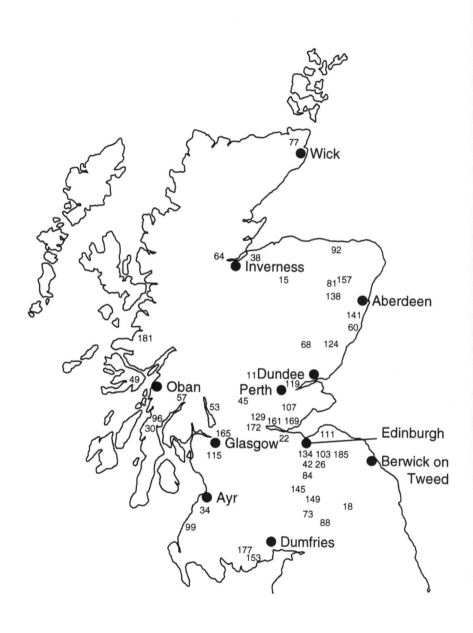

77 ● Wick

92

64 ● 38
15
Inverness

81 157
138

68 124

141
60

● Aberdeen

181

49

57
● Oban

53

96
30

45

11 Dundee ●
Perth ●
119

107

129 161 169
172

165
● Glasgow 22

115

● Ayr

34

99

● Dumfries

177
153

111

134 103 185
42 26
84

145
149
73 88
18

Edinburgh

● Berwick on
Tweed

Castle locations refer to page numbers

Aberuchill Castle and the Mail

S tanding out prominently against the green wooded slopes of the Glenartney hills two miles east of Comrie, the early nucleus of the large mansion of Aberuchill towers above the rest, a fairly typical fortalice of the early 17th century, with the usual angleturrets, stair-tower, crowstepped gables and heraldic features. Yet despite its comparative strength and the prominence of its Campbell builders, it by no means had things all its own way in Strathearn that exciting century or the next. And for this its lairds had to thank Rob Roy MacGregor.

This had been MacGregor country until the Campbells dispossessed them, and of course the MacGregors had long memories, as their motto 'My Race is Royal' implies — since this referred to no less than Alpin, King of Dalriada who died as far back as 841 and whose son was the famous Kenneth MacAlpin, who united the Picts and Scots. They descend from Kenneth's brother, and the MacGregor's proper style is Clan Alpin. Compared with this the Campbells were but upjumped newcomers. Yet we read that Colin Campbell, first of Aberuchill was granted a commission by his Chief, the seventh Earl of Argyll, Lord Justice General of Scotland, 'to apprehend and pursue to the death all persons of that most unhappie and barbarous raice of the name of MacGregor, his majesty's rebels — this to my lovit Colin Campbell of Aberuchill.' This in 1612, just after the castle was built.

So the stage was set for repercussions.

Rob Roy was the younger son of MacGregor of

Glengyle and himself laird of Inversnaid on Loch Lomondside. After the failure of the first Jacobite campaign, that of Bonnie Dundee and the collapse after Killiecrankie, Rob, who had been with his father and brothers at the battle, had to find scope for his undoubted talents and initiative — and also had to earn a living. He achieved both with considerable ingenuity and flair, getting himself appointed, of all things, Captain of the Highland Watch, a new conception of the government, to police the Highlands with a sort of territorial and part-time force — not bad for one of the defeated Jacobite 'rebels'. Then, having at his command a convenient force, naturally mainly MacGregors, he used his Watch — the forerunners of the famous Black Watch — to aid him in an elaborate system of, shall we call it, cattle-insurance, or mail, sometimes unkindly thereafter called blackmail. The notion was simplicity itself. So long as lairds and farmers paid Rob and his Watch a stipulated fee, usually in cattle, their beasts were safe from all wicked raiders and light-fingered folk. If however they refused to pay their premiums, then their cattle would be 'abstracted', nothing more certain, Rob saw to that. It was a highly

organised business, the prototype of the protection-racket and of much else in our own times.

Anyway, few landowners on the skirts of the Highlands were so foolish as to consider that they could profitably ignore Rob's system. Certainly Sir Colin Campbell, Lord Aberuchill, who had himself become Lord Justice General of Scotland, did not, and duly paid up however odd this might seem to us for one of the heads of the judiciary and a privy counsellor to boot. Especially one who had suffered losses to the extent of £17,201 Scots from the depredations of Bonnie Dundee's troops. However he was obviously a wise and discreet man; moreover, as Justice General he had been involved in setting up the Highland Watch in the first place; so perhaps he had some sympathy with the mail business. At any rate all his days he paid his dues and never lost a beast in consequence.

But, in due course he passed on like lesser men, and his son, Sir James, adopted a different attitude. Perhaps because he was the second baronet, and moreover his mother was the daughter of the Earl of Cromartie, he felt his dignity was at stake. By this time it was 1718 and the Rising known as The Fifteen had also failed, and Jacobites were no longer considered a menace. The MacGregors of course had again supported the losing Stewart side while the Campbells did the opposite. Anyway, Sir James refused to pay blackmail to a broken down Jacobite captain, little better than a cateran, and withheld his contributions for both Aberuchill and Kilbryde Castles' flocks and herds. Rob was patient and gave the laird time to pay. But to no effect. So one night as Sir James and his notable guests sat at dinner a manservant came to announce that Captain Rob Roy, formerly MacGregor, was at the castle door desiring to speak with the laird. He had told him that his master was at meat with distinguished company, but the man had declared that he must see Sir James even if the King himself was dining there that night. Rob, of course, had little respect for King William. Campbell told the servant to inform the insolent rascal that he would get nowhere with such talk and to go away before worse befell him. When the porter relayed the message, a horn sounded outside, and the servitor came hastening back to declare that MacGregor was not alone, as he had seemed to be, but had a horde of his people with him, and more were out in the surrounding parkland, shouting and hallooing. The baronet angrily went to see what went on, followed by his intrigued guests.

They found Rob Roy, in full military rig as Captain of the Watch, lounging at ease at the door, in the deepening dusk, with half of his Watch neatly drawn up in ranks behind him, the epitome of discipline and good order. Presumably it was the other half who were making all the hullaballoo out in the parks and pastures. Even as Sir James and his friends stared, the missing company coalesced and came towards the castle in an unusual formation, necessary for the droving of Aberuchill's entire stock of cattle before them, in expert fashion, to marshal them, in much mooing and snorting protest, before their owner.

Rob gave Sir James a civil good-evening, remarked on the excellence of the weather for the time of year and how illustrious was the company he was entertaining, by the looks of them, with no least mention of anything so sordid as payments of mail, ending up with a Latin tag about the better the day the better the deed — for Rob was a man of education.

Sir James advisedly took the hint, urged his guests to return to their wine, while he had a word of congratulation for the Captain of the Watch on its business-like turnout and this gesture of protection against robbers and the like.

Whether Rob was thereafter paid in cattle or in cash, the visitors could scarcely ask — but henceforward Aberuchill and Kilbryde estates' contributions arrived punctually and without fail.

Ballindalloch Castle
and Lairdly Problems

Picturesquely situated in Lower Speyside where the
River Avon coming down from the Cairngorms
joins the Spey between Grantown and Aberlour,
Ballindalloch is an interesting and imposing castle in
large wooded policies with many notable and ancient
trees, home of a famed breed of Aberdeen-Angus cattle
as well as a great family. Originally there was a line of
Ballindallochs of that Ilk; but this is Grant country, and
the Grants were not to be contained in upper Speyside;
so eventually, early in the 18th century, the Laird of Grant
from Castle Grant was in a position to give Ballindalloch
to Colonel William Grant, second son of Grant of
Rothiemurchus; and his daughter and heiress married
George Macpherson of Invereshie, near Rothiemurchus.
The resultant family, the Macpherson-Grants of
Ballindalloch, obtained a baronetcy in 1838, and produced a long line of renowned soldiers, too numerous to
recount, although the mausoleums of one of them,
General Grant, the hero of St. Lucia in 1779, is in the
neighbourhood.

There is a romantic story told of the building of the
earliest part of this castle in the mid-16th century, for it
has been greatly added to in later years. Tradition says
that it was to be erected further up the river on a more
obviously defensive site, but the work was continually
delayed by some unseen agency, the parts built during

the day always being thrown down again during the night. This greatly annoyed the laird — who would not be a Grant at this stage, for the date 1546 still appears over one of the fireplaces — until he heard a voice saying 'Build in the cow-haugh, and you shall meet with no interruptions.' The laird was impressed enough to do just that, and what was then a marshy site was accordingly chosen and the castle rose undisturbed. Marshland, of course, could be just as defensively effective as any cliff-top or promontory, in keeping invaders at bay and approachable only by an easily-guarded causeway.

Ballindalloch is a barony, and the barons used to have, among other useful privileges, the convenient one of 'pit and gallows' — that is, being able to imprison or hang without reference to a higher authority. One of the Grant lairds had reason to be wrathful at one of his own servants, recorded only by the name of Rob. Just what the crime was has not been recorded either. But summoned before the baronial court, he was duly found guilty, and was to be hanged. This Rob seems to have been a sturdy character however, and he decided to make a break for it. He kicked out at his fellow vassals who were holding him, and it looked as though he would make his escape. His wife was watching the proceedings, however, and at this juncture spoke up.

'Och, Rob — be quiet and dinna annoy the laird!' she advised.

Rob, brought to his sense of duty by this admonition, duly submitted and died like a lamb.

It is perhaps of interest how the Macpherson side of the line got its name. An ancestor, Ewan Ban, grandson of the great Gillicattan, Chief of the powerful Clan Chattan (Mackintosh) during the reign of David I in the 12th century, devoted himself to the service of the Church and became Abbot of Kingussie; which style he enjoyed until in 1155 his elder brother died childless and the Chiefship devolved upon him. He could not be both a churchman and Chief of such as Clan Chattan, and he petitioned the

Pope for a dispensation to allow him to marry. He won it, and wed the daughter of the Thane of Cawdor. His son, another Ewan, was nicknamed Macpherson, that is son of the parson; and surnames at this time becoming hereditary, so it remained.

Bemersyde and True Thomas

Romantically situated high above the River Tweed some two miles north of Dryburgh Abbey, this lofty rectangular tower-house, to which lower extensions have been added in later years to east and west, is the famed home of the Haig family. Today the oldest part looks like a fairly typical Border peel-tower of the 16th century, although the upper storey and roofline were reconstructed a century later. But undoubtedly it incorporates portions of a much earlier stronghold, for the walling is very massive, reaching a thickness of ten feet, such as was seldom built in the 16th century. The tower has open parapets only on the north and south sides, as at Smailholm Tower not far away. Originally there would be the usual 'pale' or curtain-walled enclosure around it.

The Haigs must be one of the longest-established houses in the land, settled in one spot, rather remarkable for a 'small' family; for unlike most of the great Border names, Scotts, Kerrs, Elliots, Pringles and the rest, the Haigs never seem to have spread out into subsidiary lairdships and branches. I do not recall ever having come across Haigs of anywhere else but Bemersyde until comparatively modern times. This is highly unusual for quite a prominent and renowned line.

They seem to have settled at Bemersyde from their first arrival in Scotland. They were one of the Norman families brought here by David I in the 1130s, after his long sojourn as a sort of hostage in England, where he

made so many young Norman friends. They came from the district of La Hague, in the Cotentin peninsula. We read of a Petrus de Haga of Bemersyde witnessing a charter in 1162. And a century later another Peter Haig of Bemersyde, finding that his annual payment to the monastic house of Old Melross was considered 'inappropriate' — it consisted of five fresh and five old salmon, (presumably smoked) he substituted for this the lighting during each Lent of the Chapel of St. Cuthbert there, no doubt perpetually-burning candles.

It was the only son of this laird, another Peter Haig, to whom was made the Rhymer prophesy, soon after, when his father had just died, which has made Bemersyde famous down the ages. Sir Thomas Learmonth of Ercildoune, better known as True Thomas or Thomas the Rhymer, perhaps Scotland's first major poet — and of course a seer or soothsayer of great renown — was a neighbour of the Haigs, Ercildoune being the old name for what is now Earlston, a mere four miles from Bemersyde. They were, in fact, both vassals of the powerful Earls of Dunbar and March, from whom Earlston takes its name. Well, poor Peter Haig was blessed with five of a family, but unfortunately all were daughters. The new laird had to have his lands duly confirmed to him by charter from his superior, the Earl; and it so happened that Sir Thomas was present when this deed fell to be signed and witnessed. The charter confirmed the lands of Bemersyde to Petrus de Haga, the Latinised form, and to the heirs male of his body in lawful succession — the usual phraseology. Haig, of course was exceedingly sensitive about all these daughters and no son, although he had been married for almost 20 years; it was indeed something of a joke locally. Now, at this signing-session, he gloomily declared that, despite the charter, it looked as though he would in fact be the last Haig of Bemersyde. It was then that Thomas the Rhymer came to his rescue and prophesied:

> *Time and tide, what may betide*
> *Haig will be Haig of Bemersyde.*

And, of course, so great was the soothsayer's fame and folk's faith in his predictions, that Haig, the Earl and the other witnesses, had no least doubts that the line of Haig was now assured. Presumably Peter went home to his good lady and dealt with her in suitable fashion, as an act of faith. At any rate, in due course, she became pregnant again and bore the required son and heir, amidst great rejoicings.

From that day to this there have been Haigs at Bemersyde.

Mind you, it sometimes seems to have been touch-and-go. The grandfather of the laird in Walter Scott's time, for instance, produced no fewer than 12 daughters before buoyed up presumably by the Rhymer's prophesy, he and his long-suffering partner, tried once more, and won. And, as Scott puts it, the common people trembled for the credit of their favourite soothsayer, but were reassured.

Then there was the difficult case of James, the seventeenth, a character described as of turbulent and vindictive temper. He made a runaway marriage with the daughter of the Laird of Stodrig, which so upset his father that he drew his dirk to stab him — which seems to indicate that the temper might have been hereditary. He was disinherited, but the marriage was fruitful, to the extent of producing ten sons. Yet his brother William, who became Laird instead, and held the office of King's Solicitor for Scotland, for James VI, produced no offspring at all. Thirsting for revenge, his brother James accused the Solicitor-General of treason, and both brothers were locked up in Edinburgh Tolbooth until William was able to clear his name. This was 1616. James seems to have been forgiven, and fled to Germany, where he died in 1620, 'for hungry ruin had him in the wind'.

William Haig having no descendants, Bemersyde had to go to someone, and he chose his nephew David, James's seventh son. This was rather hard on his eldest brother Robert, who after all was the Haig's true heir. As it happened, however, Robert's line got its own back in the end. For he it was who started the whisky-distilling enterprise, at St. Ninians, near Stirling, and from him descended the famous whisky Haigs in Fife, who eventually produced General Sir Douglas Haig, the First World War commander. And we all know how, in 1921, when the incumbent Haig of Bemersyde stock appeared to be on the way out at long last, a grateful nation bought the estate from Lt Colonel A. Balfour Haig and presented it to the General, and he was created Earl Haig of Bemersyde, Order of Merit. Today his son, a noted artist, the second Earl Haig, lives in the old tower above the Tweed, and he has a son.

Blackness Castle
and its Prisoners

It is rather extraordinary that this fine castle, a royal fortress never in private hands, within 20 miles of Edinburgh, is so little known. Few people with whom I have spoken of it have known of its existence. Yet it is both good to look at and has a resounding history.

Blackness stands on a little headland jutting out into the Firth of Forth four miles north-east of Linlithgow in West Lothian, below the better-known estate of The Binns. There is a small village, anciently the port of Linlithgow. The castle, thought by some experts to mark the eastern extremity of the Antonine Wall of the Romans, is an imposing and substantial place shaped

like a ship within its curtain-walls, nowadays kept in good repair and still belonging to the Crown. In fact it was one of the chief forts of Scotland, specifically guaranteed by the Act of Union of 1707 to be maintained permanently as a national strength.

Blackness has served various purposes and undergone odd vicissitudes in its long story. Just when it was first built is not known, but it was burned and seriously damaged in 1443-4 during the upheavals when the Douglases, Crichtons and Livingstones were tearing the kingdom apart between them to control the Crown. This was only its first conflagration for it was restored and then burned again by an English fleet in 1481, in the troubled reign of James III. Again rebuilt, it served as the chosen meeting-place for James and his rebellious lords in 1488. It is recorded that the sight of such numbers of his most important subjects, all arrayed for mortal combat, and having in their power his elder son — who the same year became James IV — so upset this unwarlike monarch that he agreed to humiliating terms under what became known as the pacification of Blackness. Later he was persuaded to go back on his word — a situation which ended in the fatal Battle of Sauchieburn that year and the death of the King.

Amongst the many great ones incarcerated here was Cardinal David Beaton of St. Andrews in 1542, Primate of Scotland and later Chancellor, while he was holding up the Reformation movement in Scotland. He was committed to the custody of the Lord Seton, father of the one who was to rescue Mary Queen of Scots from Loch Leven. As a reprisal, the spirited Cardinal-Archbishop ordered from Blackness that all religious services were to be suspended throughout the land during his imprisonment, all priests to refuse baptism and Christian burial, all churches to be closed and so on — a drastic situation which produced the greatest consternation in the still-Catholic Scotland and undoubtedly hastened Beaton's release, although Henry VIII of England, who was trying to force the Reformation on Scotland, was demanding that the Cardinal be handed over to him for confinement in an English prison. Even the Scots Protestant lords found this too much to swallow and Beaton's escape from Blackness was facilitated.

Five years later, still during Henry's Rough Wooing period of Mary Queen of Scots' infancy, Blackness was the scene of an assault by an English fleet under Lord Clinton — presumably the same which attacked Luffness Castle that same year, trying to raise the Siege of Haddington — and although the invaders did not manage to take the castle here, they burned or captured no fewer than ten vessels in the port of Blackness, an indication that its reputation to have been the third port of Scotland at this period may well have been true. The English chronicler's account of this action makes lively reading:

> *My Lord Clynton, hye Admiral of this flete, taking with him the galley (whereof one Broke is Captain) and iiii or v of our smaller vessels besides, all well appointed with municion and men, rowed up the frith a ten myle westward, to a haven towne standying on the south shore called Blacknestes, whereat, towards the water syde is a castel of a pretty strength. As nigh whear unto as the depth of water thear woold suffer, the Skots, for savegard, had laied ye Mary Willoughby and the Antony of Newcastel, ii tall ships, whiche with extreme injury they had stollen from us before tyme, whe no war between us; with these ley thear also an oother large vessel called (by them) the Brosse, and a vii mo, whereof part laden with merchandize. My Lord Clynton and his copenie, wt right hardy approce, after a great conflict betwixt the castel and our vessels, by fyne force, wan from them those iii ships of name and burnt all ye residue before their faces as they ley.*

Strangely, in a reversal of fortunes, Blackness Castle was in the hands of Mary's supporters in 1572 and holding out against the Protestant lords. But it was lost a year later when Sir James Kirkcaldy, brother of the more famous Kirkcaldy of Grange who held Edinburgh Castle for the Queen, landed here from France with a large supply of money and military stores for the garrison and Mary's cause. But he was betrayed — by his own wife it is said — and seized, along with his stores and money and the castle itself, during the landing and transporting process. This put the notorious Regent Morton in command.

Twenty years later in 1592, came the dire business of the slaying of the Bonnie Earl o' Moray at Donibristle, subject of the famous ballad, the Earl of Huntly being villain of the piece. Moray had been popular, and whatever James VI's implication in the matter, he advised that Huntly put himself in voluntary ward in Blackness Castle until the furore died down. This Huntly did, and managed to live there in entire comfort; and in due course, after the merest cosmetic investigation, was found innocent of all but a mistake of judgement, pardoned and released.

Blackness was not yet finished with its excitements and sorrows, for it became a convenient state prison, like the Bass Rock and Dunottar Castle, for distinguished Covenanters in their time of persecution.

In somewhat more recent times, the castle became a barracks and then the central ammunition depot for Scotland. Even in the later 19th century it was staffed by a governor, a lieutenant-governor, two gunners, one sergeant and fourteen privates — sounding rather like the Grand Army of Mexico!

Borthwick Castle under Assault

B orthwick is perhaps the most splendid peel-tower in all Scotland, a huge and massive keep no less than 110 feet high, standing within its curtain-walls on a shelf in the valley of the Gore Water two miles south-east of Gorebridge, in Midlothian. It was built by the first Lord Borthwick about 1430 and is still in the hands of that ancient family, having survived the impact of the centuries intact — or almost so. And they have been fairly impactful centuries.

Borthwick's stories start from the very beginning, as stories should, for when Lord Borthwick bought Locherworth, sometimes spelt Lochquhariat, from its Hay laird, built his mighty castle and named it Borthwick instead of Locherworth, Laird Hay, thought that this was bad form, unsuitable. So, since he had not sold the land on the other, eastern side of the Gore Water, he built a mill thereon, at the nearest point under the castle walls, so that the everlasting clack of its mill-wheel would keep the new lord awake of a night and remind him that siller power could not buy everything.

Of all the Borthwick stories, my favourite is the one about Mary Queen of Scots, that marvellous fountain of tales and anecdotes. The Queen came here in 1567 with Bothwell, whom she had just made Duke of Orkney, as guests of the sixth lord. The Confederate Lords, who hated Bothwell, Morton, Home, Mar and the rest, got to hear of it and came in force to apprehend him. Warned in time, the new Duke managed to get away before the others arrived to encircle the castle — but, not very gallantly perhaps, left the Queen behind. Presumably he thought that she was in no danger from these extreme Protestant subjects.

Anyway, Mary herself appears to have thought differently, for she decided to slip away, if she could, and rejoin Bothwell. Waiting until darkness, she dressed herself in the clothing of a page, young Borthwick of Crookston, and had herself lowered on a rope from the great hall window on the first floor. Thereafter, alone, she made her way through the confederate lines in the darkness and across the foothills to Cakemuir Castle, three miles away, whither Bothwell also had gone — her room is still pointed out there. It made an extraordinary interlude in the life of a reigning queen and throws a significant light on her spirited character and physical stamina — as did the famous ride to Hermitage Castle a year before; even though Bothwell does not seem to come quite so well out of it.

There was a modern sequel to this, for me. I was asked

to act as historical adviser for a feature on Mary in the French magazine, *Marie France*, some years ago, and had to pinpoint all the locations of the Queen's activities and also to find someone to act the part of Mary for the photographer — an actress, they suggested. I did not know of any suitable actresses, but I introduced them to the very good-looking Margaret Hope of Luffness, my own laird's daughter, who is descended from Mary on both her mother's and father's sides. And dressed in a variety of gowns for the period, brought from France specially, Margaret duly performed many of the spectacular incidents in her ancestress's life, including this lowering on a rope from Borthwick Castle's window in page's clothing, a sufficiently hair-raising performance, the camera recording all. I take my hat off to both ladies.

A third story must suffice for Borthwick. Cromwell came here in 1650, on business bent. Ringing round the castle with his troops, he actually sent the eighth Lord Borthwick a letter thus:

I thought fitt to send this trumpett to you, to lett you know that, if you please to walk away with your company ... you shall have liberties to carry off your arms and goods and such other necessaries as you have. You harboured such parties in your house as have basely unhumanely murdered our men; if you necessitate me to bend my cannon against you, you must expect what I doubt you will not be pleased with. I expect your present answer, and rest your servant,

O. Cromwell

Not getting any reply to this O. Cromwell accordingly opened fire with his heavy artillery, and although these did not manage to breach the immensely thick walling — 14 feet thick at the foot and six feet at parapet level — the cannon-balls did make a sufficient dent in the castle, still very visible, for its lord to decide that in this instance discretion might be the better part of valour. So he sent word to the Lord Protector that he saw the point; and Cromwell very courteously not only allowed Lord and Lady Borthwick with their family and retainers to march off unmolested, but even gave them an additional 15 days to remove their effects before occupying the castle with his troops. One feels that all concerned came quite well out of this one.

Incidentally during the last war, a great many of the precious documents of Scotland were stored in the vaults and the chambers of this great castle, for safe keeping against air-raids.

Carnassery Castle
and the Big Man

An Carselach Mor in Carnasserie,
There are five quarters * to his hose;
His rump is like the back of a crane,
His stomach is empty, greedy and sadly capacious.

This verse, translated from the Gaelic, is illuminating in more ways than one. The character thus described was the builder of this castle, one of the finest and most ambitious in all the Highlands, in its day. It stands, ruinous now, but in the care of the Department of the Environment, and tolerably entire, on high ground above the main A816 road from Lochgilphead to Oban, near the head of the Kilmartin valley just a little way north of where the A840 branches off eastwards for Loch Awe.

Its story is unusual, to say the least, for this massive stronghold was erected, not by any great lord or clan chief but by a churchman and a Reformer at that — of a sort: John Carsewell is the name he goes by in the historybooks, but probably this was not his true name. Much more likely it was John or Ian Campbell, for he was the son of the Earl of Argyll's Constable of an earlier Carnassery, and of the smaller Kilmartin Castle only two miles to the south — and MacCailean Mor of Argyll was

---

*45 inches

apt to see to it that the keepers of his castles were good and reliable Campbells. John was born at Kilmartin Castle in the first half of the 16th century. The verse calls him An Carselach Mor, which just means 'the big man of the carse' — carse meaning fertile low ground flanking a river, in this case the Kilmartin Water. Carsewell would be merely an approximate anglicisation of his Gaelic byname.

At any rate, when we first hear of him, before 1560, he was Rector of Kilmartin, in Holy Church, the Reformation being somewhat slow at reaching Argyll; and living in his family home in the modest castle, which still remains, ruinous also but fairly complete, above the village of Kilmartin. He seems to have been a huge man of Herculean frame and great energy and ability, but agile of character if not of person, and an eminent scholar into the bargain. This was of course a lively period in both religious and political matters, the reign of Mary Queen of Scots, when the Reformation was touch-and-go. Carsewell seems to have been seized with Reforming zeal — or at least, saw the light of opportunity — for he

surged ahead in the new Kirk but in a strangely equivo-
cal fashion, becoming in 1560 one of the new
Superintendents who replaced the bishops, in this case of
Argyll and the Isles, a highiy significant position; but
also, oddly, styling himself Abbot of Iona, which does not
sound especially reformed. He further distinguished
himself by translating and publishing John Knox's
Liturgy, in Gaelic, a compendium of the doctrines of the
Presbyterian faith, the first book ever published in the
Gaelic language.

Despite the enthusiasm for Presbyterianism, however,
within a year he was attending a parliament in
Edinburgh, sitting and accepting the style and title of
Bishop of Argyll and the Isles, nominated as such by
Queen Mary. He managed to get an enactment passed
that one Lachlan McLean must renounce all rights to the
said bishopric of Argyll and the Isles and the abbacy of
Iona and was bound not to molest John Carsewell in possession of the same. He also obtained from the Crown the
lucrative post of Chancellor of the Chapel-Royal of
Stirling. So obviously the Reformation was at this stage
not entirely a fait accompli, and it paid an astute cleric to
be nimble — especially as he was in process of building
a quite magnificent castle, commensurate with his new
power and status, just up the glen. To be on the safe side,
too, Carnassery's thick walls were well supplied with
shot-holes and splayed gunloops and other stout
defences — although the Bishop did not neglect ele-
gance, heraldic decoration and godly Gaelic inscriptions.

But Mary's cause went down and another parliament,
in 1568, enacted that no-one, as churchmen, should have
power to vote save Superintendents, bishops again
becoming anathema. So John had to change his style
once more; and in fact he was censured by the next
General Assembly of the Kirk for having accepted the
Queen's bishopric. It was all very difficult for a well-
doing Campbell.

However, An Carselach Mor seems to have ridden out

this storm, as so many another, and continued with his ambitious building work — and indeed, continued to call himself Bishop of the Isles, at least here in his own Argyll until his death in 1572. Curiously, for some reason, he was not buried among his own folk in the fine kirkyard of Kilmartin, but in distant Ardchattan Priory on the shore of Loch Etive. It is perhaps significant that this great Campbell religious centre was very reluctant to embrace Reformed status and in fact it was not until 1600 that the last Prior, Alexander Campbell, finally secularised Ardchattan. So perhaps that is why John Carsewell chose to rest his mighty frame there at last, a Catholic in the end?

Carnassery passed to another branch of the Campbell clan, that of Auchinbreck, but sadly was blown up during the Argyll Rising of 1685.

Cassillis House and
the Kings of Carrick

The so-called Kings of Carrick, the Earls of Cassillis by name, were Chiefs of the Kennedys, and an autocratic lot they were. This was their main seat, acquired in 1372 by marriage with the Montgomerie heiress, their previous stronghold having been the savage Dunure Castle, on the coast not far away. They were Celtic, descended from the old Pictish Lords of Galloway. Cassillis stands in a strong position above the River Doon, the same Burns wrote about, some four miles north-east of Maybole, the Carrick and Kennedy 'capital'. It consists of a great and massive oblong keep, probably of the late 14th century, which was somewhat altered and extended in the 17th century and gained more additions in more modern times. But the original mighty tower, with walls no less than 14 feet thick at base, still dominates all and speaks proudly of the power and prestige of the Kings of Carrick.

The Kennedys flourished not only in Carrick and all Ayrshire and Galloway, but on a national scale, and sent out innumerable branches from the main stem at Cassillis. The grandson of the one who married Cassillis aspired higher, and wed the Princess Margaret, daughter of Robert III. Their son was one of the six Regents of Scotland during the minority of James III, and became first Lord Kennedy. The third Lord was created Earl of Cassillis, and fell at Flodden. Flaming Janet Kennedy, sister of the first Earl, was the renowned and beautiful mistress of James IV — who, being married to the curious Margaret Tudor, sister of Henry VIII and of a similar character, no doubt deserved a kindly mistress. At any rate the King attained a great reputation for piety by frequently going on pilgrimage to St. Ninian's shrine at Whithorn in Galloway, on which trips it was convenient to stop overnight with Janet, at Cassillis, going and coming; and it is noteworthy that when later he installed Janet, with their infant son, in Darnaway Castle in Moray, he changed his saintly allegiance to St. Duthac at Tain, in Ross, to which Darnaway made a convenient halfway-house.

Of all the many dramas connected with Cassillis probably the two most telling are the Crossraguel Roast and the Auchendrane Tragedy, both occurring in that most exdting hundred years in Scotland's long story between 1550 and 1650. The Crossraguel affair dates from 1570 and concerns Gilbert, fourth Earl, 'a very greedy man' by

repute. It so happened that the nearby Cluniac abbey of Crossraguel, founded by one of the Earl's ancestors in 1240, and which the Kennedys had looked upon practically as their own property with a long succession of Kennedy abbots, somehow at the Reformation carve-up went to one Allan Stewart, as Commendator-Abbot, with all its lands and riches. No doubt he had useful Stewart links with the Crown. It should perhaps be explained that these new secular owners of Church lands and monasteries continued to be called Commendator-Abbots and Priors although Protestants and having no religious functions, this because most of the abbeys and priories held age-old seats in the Scots parliament, and other privileges, which their new owners were loth to relinquish.

At any rate, the Earl of Cassillis, whose uncle Quentin Kennedy had been the last genuine abbot, was not amused. On a visit by the new Commendator to his domains, the Earl had him kidnapped and taken to Dunure Castle, not Cassillis, and there, in the Black Vault, when Stewart refused to oblige him, had the unfortunate man 'roasted in sop' on a slow fire until in desperation he agreed 'to sign a five-year tack and a 19-year tack and charged to feu all the lands of Crossraguel, with all the clauses necessar, for the great King of Carrick to haste him to hell!'

This presumably was Stewart's version of the agreement. I have heard of no record nor suggestion that this contract was ever repudiated nor any reprisal in law executed against the Earl.

It was this Earl's son, John, Lord Treasurer of Scotland, who was responsible for the affair in 1601, which Walter Scott has made famous by his work *Auchendrane* or the *Ayrshire Tragedy*, and it had its links with the Crossraguel business. The Earl, at the head of two hundred armed followers, waylaid Mure of Bargany, a neighbour, and forced on him a wholly unequal conflict.

Mortally wounded, Bargany was carried from the

scene of the onset, at West Enoch, to Maybole, where, should he show any signs of recovery, he might be despatched by Cassillis as Judge Ordinary of the area. By skilful diplomacy the Earl not only went unpunished but managed to get the Privy Council to commend it as an act of good service to the realm. The Laird of Auchendrane, son-in-law of the victim, and wounded in the fight, however pursued his own vengeance and managed in turn to waylay and slay Sir Thomas Kennedy of Culzean, an uncle of the Earl. The resultant barbarities and treacheries made the theme of Scott's *Tragedy*.

Cawdor Castle — such Stuff as Dreams are made ...

Hail to thee Thane of Glamis!
Hail to thee, Thane of Cawdor!

Historically, Shakespeare may not have been very accurate about MacBeth for he was Mormaor of Moray and Ross before he became King, a much more lofty position than Thane of Cawdor or Glamis. Nevertheless, Cawdor was a name of ancient importance, with its own drama, sufficient for any playwright. And the present handsome castle is certainly of the stuff woven from the yarn of high romance.

In this case, even the founding of the castle is unusually dramatic. The story goes that in 1454 the then Thane Calder — Cawdor being merely the North-East's way of pronouncing and spelling Calder — received a licence from the Crown to build and fortify a private castle. Up till then the thanes, who claimed to be of the family of MacBeth — which is presumably where Shakespeare got it — had occupied the royal stronghold of Nairn as hereditary constables; and still their descendants hold the Constabulary House there. At any rate, this Calder went about the business of erecting a new castle in unique fashion. He dreamed a dream about it. In this, he was instructed to load a chest of gold on to the back of a donkey and then to turn the animal loose. Needless to say, even in a dream he was not to say goodbye to the

donkey or gold but to keep the brute in sight, following it wherever it went. It would wander about and feed here and there, but it was not to be interfered with. But when it finally stopped and lay down, there was to be the site of the new castle. Exactly there and nowhere else was the building to be erected — and if all this was complied with, the house and its owners would be blessed indeed.

The Thane, who must have been a man of unusual parts, did just as he had dreamed, loaded an unspecified amount of gold on a donkey and let it loose, to follow on at a discreet distance. It seems to have been a wander-some creature, for it went hither and thither for much of the day, without apparent objective save for delectable thistles, which must have been taxing indeed on Calder's patience. However, towards evening, no doubt feeling the weight of the chest of gold, the animal eventually sank down to rest beneath a hawthorn-tree on rising ground above a bend in a burn's ravine, and, despite all the to-ing and fro-ing, a mere five miles south by west from where it had set out at Nairn. And precisely there the Thane in due course built Cawdor Castle.

You may well raise an eyebrow at this tale, judging it picturesque but improbable. Nevertheless, if you visit Cawdor Castle do not fail to look into the vaulted basement chamber of the old square keep. And there, in the centre, you will see a tree growing out of the floor. Not only so but it continues up and disappears through the ancient masonry of the arched roof, this most obviously having been built to incorporate the topmost branches. The tree is dead now, of course, but substantial and clearly a hawthorn. In inspecting a thousand castles, I have never seen the like.

If you remain a disbeliever, there is still much in Cawdor's story to capture your attention. Not so very long after the castle was built, in 1499, the Thane's son and successor, Iain Calder, died, leaving as heiress only a four-year-old daughter named Muriella. I never heard of a thane-ess, but at least Muriella Calder inherited castle and lands, although her father left sundry brothers, her uncles. Heiresses were always in great demand — still are, I imagine — and there was no lack of ambitious suitors for the little red-haired girl's hand. But the Campbells, on this occasion, did more than merely press their suit and make the legal aggressions for which they were famous. The second Earl of Argyll sent Campbell of Inverliver, on Loch Aweside, all the way across Scotland to Nairnshire actually to collect the heiress willy-nilly and bring her to Innishonnel Castle — which was the chief Campbell seat before Inveraray — also on Loch Awe. Inverliver went well prepared and escorted, needless to say by his party including his own seven sons.

They seem to have rather caught the Calders napping, for they managed to extract Muriella from Cawdor Castle, despite all its defences, without too much trouble and set off with her on the long road south-westwards to Argyll. But, in due course, the uncles gathered their wits and their clansmen and gave chase. I estimate that it is about 200 miles from Cawdor to Loch Awe, by the most direct routes, so there was plenty of opportunity for the pursuit to catch up. This it did more than once, and was either beaten off or eluded. However, matters for the kidnappers were beginning to look grim when Inverliver devised a cunning, albeit expensive, plan. After a brief halt for refreshment, he arranged for a large cauldron, used as a sort of outsize camp-kettle, to be inverted, and this guarded to the death by his seven devoted sons, while he dashed off with the four-year-old. It is perhaps interesting that the fleeing Campbells should have retained so large and cumbersome an item of equipment for thus long. However the device worked. The Calders duly presumed that their heiress was hidden underneath the pot and the seven young men sold their lives dearly and with sufficient delay to allow their father and prize to get clean away. When it was later suggested that if the little girl should die, the loss of his sons would be a heavy price to pay, Inverliver is reputed to have replied that Muriella Calder could never die so long as a red-haired lassie could be found on Loch Aweside. Presumably a little surgical amputation would also have been called for in such circumstances, for the child's nurse is alleged to have bitten off the top joint of her little finger, in the cause of permanent identification, during the bustle of capture.

As postscript, of course, it falls to be recorded that 11 years later Muriella was duly married to Sir John Campbell, third son of the Earl of Argyll. And the Campbells, in the shape of the sixth Earl Cawdor, still hold Cawdor. Stirring days!

If all this is not enough to recommend this splendid castle to you, it is perhaps worth mentioning that the famous Lord Lovat hid here after the collapse of the Forty-Five rising, in a remarkable secret chamber contrived in the roofing. I could go on further but will not.

Craigmillar Castle and
a Royal Treachery

Set on its lofty ridge, and dominating the south-eastern suburbs of Edinburgh, Craigmillar Castle is certainly not to be overlooked. It is a major stronghold in size and strength, as it is in story, and played a large part in Scotland's affairs down the centuries, being first recorded in the early 13th century. It is unusual in that, although it was always in private ownership, it nevertheless served as a semi-royal establishment during many reigns, much used as a sort of adjunct to Edinburgh Castle and Holyroodhouse. It was particularly useful for the royal household to retire to when plague struck the city, as it frequently did.

The Prestons of Craigmillar were from 1374 and for long after the lairds here, the family playing a prominent part in the life of Edinburgh as well as further afield, as provosts, magistrates, judges and the like. Sir Simon Preston was much involved in Mary Queen of Scots' affairs, he being the Provost. Mary herself was frequently in residence here, so much so that the neighbouring hamlet to the west, useful for lodging her train of courtiers, so many of them French, gained the name of Little France, and still is so-called. At Craigmillar her divorce from Henry, Lord Darnley, was first suggested to her by Bothwell, her half-brother the Earl of Moray, the Earl of Argyll, the Earl of Huntly and Secretary Lethington. This became known as the Craigmillar Conference. Darnley was later slain at Kirk o' Field, although it had been proposed that he should be brought to this castle — a murky business. How much of it all the Queen was aware, is debatable.

But a royal ancestor of Mary's, James III, was largely responsible for an even more unsavoury event. James, a weak monarch, was much under the influence of unscrupulous favourites, notably Archbishop Sheves of St. Andrews, an astrologer and so-called magician who gained his high office in the Church by very dubious means. Sheves and the other favourites found their machinations being countered by the King's two brothers, Alexander, Duke of Albany and John, Earl of Mar, both much more effective characters than the monarch. James was persuaded to have them arrested. Albany was confined in Edinburgh Castle, but John of Mar was sent to Craigmillar for imprisonment. Albany managed to contrive an escape from the citadel, and fled the country; but Mar was less fortunate. After a period of captivity, under the pretext that he was ill, he was conveyed back to Edinburgh in the care of the King's physician and taken to a house in the Canongate where, allegedly in the interests of his health, he was 'bled'. But this was an especial bleeding. He was placed in a bath of warm water, and

there his veins cut open, and he was held down until he bled to death. Thus it could all be accounted for as but a well-meant attempt which went wrong. However, rumours quickly spread, so to help cover up the murder a number of unfortunate women were rounded up and accused of witchcraft and conspiring with Mar to encompass the King's death by means of spells and incantations. They were burned at the stake.

In happier vein, James V spent much time at Craigmillar as a youth, being tutored by Gavin Dunbar and instructed in outdoor pursuits by his page, Sir David Lindsay of the Mount, who later became the famous Lord Lyon King of Arms, and composed, among other epics, *Ane Satyre of the Thrie Estaits*. Later in the child Mary's reign in 1544, the English Earl of Hertford, sent by Henry VIII, invaded by sea with a fleet of 200 ships, attacking Edinburgh and doing much damage. He could not take the great fortress-castle however, and so chose to assail Craigmillar instead. This in due course was forced to surrender, on terms that it remained 'scatheless', which was agreed. But on gaining it, Hertford promptly ordered it to be burned — although, of course, these stone castles were not so easily consumed by fire.

It was however restored, and Mary Queen of Scots' son, James VI used Craigmillar much. It was here that he is said to have planned his marriage to Anne of Denmark and devised his journey to that country, an expedition which, to the consternation of his ministers, lasted considerably longer than anticipated — but then, Jamie the Saxt was apt to be that always.

Craigmillar Castle is now in good care and open to the public.

Doune Castle and the Bonnie Earl

O lang will his lady,
Look owre the Castle Doune,
Ere she sees the Earl O' Moray,
Come sounding through the toun.

We all know the famous and resounding ballad, but not all understand its fullest implications perhaps, or the references to Castle Doune and the town; for the action in the said tale takes place elsewhere, in Edinburgh and Linlithgow and Fife, not in the Menteith area of Perthshire.

The castle, one of the finest and most imposing in the land, tall and massive, with its huge gatehouse-keep and lofty curtain-walls still entire, stands on an eminence above the junction of the Ardoch Burn and the River Teith, quite near the delightful little town of the same name, open to the public and a place to visit. And the Earl of Moray's son still bears the courtesy-title of Lord Doune, although he does not now live in this castle, but not far away.

What, I have found, is not always realised is that in the ballad the lady who looks owre the Castle Doune is not the Earl of Moray's countess-wife but his mother, the Lady Doune, which admittedly seems strange.

The story, of course, goes thus. The Earl of Moray, handsome, gallant and an ornament to James VI's court, had succeeded his father, a Stewart, as Lord Doune. But on marrying the daughter of the Regent Moray, Mary

Queen of Scots's half-brother who was assassinated at Linlithgow, gained with her the earldom of Moray, the Regent leaving no son. The young man's good looks and flourish appealed to the ladies, and these included the Queen, Anne of Denmark. There was almost certainly nothing reprehensible about their association, however romantic-sounding the ballad makes it; however, King James became jealous — for he was anything but handsome and gallant, slobbery-mouthed, his tongue too big for his mouth, and knock-kneed, even though the Wisest Fool in Christendom. The King resented Moray's accomplishments, at sports, tournaments, on the dance-floor and in other aspects of court life. And Jamie the Saxt was a bad enemy to have.

Unfortunately Moray had another enemy — or at least one who coveted not his prowess at court but his great lands in the North, some of which had formerly been in the coveter's family — the Cock o' the North himself, the Gordon Chief, the Earl of Huntly. And he was unscrupulous as he was powerful. For his own purpose he poisoned the King's mind against Moray, suggesting treachery, even treason, as well as undue influence with the Queen. He won James's permission to take such measures as he saw fit, even though the monarch was later to protest:

'I bade you bring him wi' you
And forbade you him to slay.'

But Huntly contrived Moray's death at Donibristle in Fife, another of his seats, by setting fire to the castle and, when Moray managed to get out, his hair allegedly alight, he was struck down by the Gordons, in a ghastly scene. One of Huntly's lairds, Gordon of Buckie, seems to have been foremost in this shameful business but, concerned that he might be given any blame for the assassination, insisted that his Chief at least deliver one blow in front of all. Whereupon Huntly drew his dirk and

slashed it across Moray's face, occasioning the dying man's famous last words: 'You, Huntly — you have spoiled a better face than your own!'

There was of course, a major reaction. Uproar swept the nation. Popular anger manifested itself against Huntly, the leading Catholic in the land, and the whole Catholic interest suffered. But fingers everywhere also pointed at the King. James, who was no hero, immediately declared himself innocent. He tried to cover it all up, and when he was unsuccessful in that, made a pretext of punishing Huntly by confining him in the state prison of Blackness Castle near Linlithgow, but with every comfort, all his Gordon henchmen to attend him, a mere gesture.

It was now that Lady Doune, the mother, comes into the picture. She was a Campbell, Margaret, daughter of the 4th Earl of Argyll, and a strong-minded woman — which presumably the young Countess of Moray up in Darnaway Castle was not, for we hear nothing of her.

47

The mother adopted her own methods as to exposure and revenge. Indeed exposure was the word, for she had her son's naked, stabbed and mutilated body installed in the Kirk of Leith for all to see, burial deferred; and had the Earl's blood-stained shirt paraded through Edinburgh's streets, while she demanded vengeance and aroused continuing storm against the King and Huntly. James, no hero, scuttled off to Glasgow for a period until things died down, something he was far from wont to do.

Huntly, presently, was allowed to retire quietly to his northern territories, no other action taken — but he did not then get the coveted Moray lands.

However, who knows who won in the end? For, having declared that he 'did nothing but by His Majesty's commission and so was neither art or part in the murder', James, no doubt to keep Huntly's mouth shut in future, persuaded the new Earl of Moray, only five at his father's death, to marry Lady Anne Gordon. Which satisfactorily closed the chapter, did it not?

> *'He was a braw gallant,*
> *And he rid at the ring;*
> *And the bonnie Earl o' Moray,*
> *Oh he might have been a King.'*

Duart Castle and the Clan Spirit

Proudly crowning its lofty rock-headland jutting into Duart Bay, off the Sound of Mull — Duart is just Dubh Ard, the Dark Headland — this must be everyone's notion of what a Highland chieftain's stronghold should look like, strong indeed, picturesque, romantic. Nor, on closer inspection and investigation, does Duart fail in any respect to sustain first impressions. It is in fact the seat and home of the 28th Chief of Clan Gillean, Sir Lachlan Maclean of Duart and Morvern. Long ruinous, it was restored by the present Chief's great-grandfather, Sir Fitzroy Maclean, who purchased it in 1911 and restored it into a most attractive house, full of treasures and a worthy shrine for its crowding memories.

What stories these ancient walls could tell, we can only hint at. The clan takes its name from a 13th-century paladin known as Gillean of the Battle Axe, descended through the house of Lorn from the Dalriadic King of Scots, and linked by marriage to the Lords of the Isles, from whom spring also the MacDonalds and Mac-Dougalls and others. The Macleans were long a major support for the great Lordship and involved in all its many excitements.

The present castle dates from the end of the 14th century, built by Lachlan Lubanach (or the Wily) Maclean, on the site of a still earlier stronghold. This Chief had to obtain special Papal dispensation from Rome to make possible his marriage to Mary, daughter of the Lord of the Isles, his cousin. This seems to have been an altogether dramatic match — the pair being sufficiently in love and the lady having the reputation of 'an inclination for yielding' — that her father's permission was only gained by Maclean kidnapping him. However, in the stramash the Chief of Clan Mackinnon was unfortunately killed. Despite this unconventional start all seems to have worked out in the end — except for poor Mackinnon — and Lachlan the Wily grew in favour with his father-in-law, who presumably had a sneaking approval for strong-arm tactics, for he gave him the former Mackinnon lands on Mull and Duart thus arose. Such was life on the Hebridean coastline.

Tales could be told, I suppose, of practically every one of these spirited Chiefs, but two must suffice. First the extraordinary story of the rivalry between the two branches of Clan Gillean, these Macleans of Duart and their kinsmen the Maclaines (these insisted even on spelling their name differently) of Lochbuie. With

Lochbuie's castle of Moy just over the hill, this was an astonishing but very continuing situation.

For some reason, however, in the mid-16th century, Hector Mor Maclean of Duart actually supported his opposite number Ian the Toothless of Lochbuie in countering an attempt by Ian's own son, Ewan of the Little Head, to take over the Maclaine power. Chieftains, I suppose, had to seem to stick together. In this family quarrel Ewan lost his little head, and his ghost, known as the Headless Horseman, is said to ride whenever a Maclaine of Lochbuie is dying. Be that as it may, this did not finish the incident, for having got rid of Ewan the heir, Hector of Duart then rounded up the father, Toothless Ian — which, I imagine, may well have been intended all along — and although he did not kill him, took him out to the remote, uninhabited Treshnish isle of Caimburgh and there marooned him with only an elderly and ugly female servant as companion. This, no doubt, was to ensure that there would be no further heirs to complicate matters in the Maclean-Maclaine dynasty, for Ian had no sons other than the late Ewan. Needless to say, Hector Mor saw to it that there was no rescue for the unfortunate Toothless Ian, as the time went on.

However, in due course, the unlikely mother bore a son, and when Ian died — probably from eating too many shellfish — the woman was allowed to go. Wisely she had kept the child's birth a secret, and she managed to smuggle the boy out with her and escaped with him to Ireland. There Murdoch the Stunted grew up and eventually came back to Mull and won over Lochbuie from Hector Mor's son.

The second tale concerns the well-known Lady Rock in the Sound of Mull. Lachlan Cattanach Maclean of Duart, tiring of his Campbell wife, marooned her on this tidal rock, which one can still see at low water from the Oban-Craignure ferry. Obviously the Maclean mind ran on marooning. Only this was not intended to be a lengthy immolation, for the rock was covered at high tide. However, unknown to the Maclean, the lady was rescued by some homing fisherman, and on making it known she was a sister to no less than Macailean Mor himself, she was promptly taken to that potent Earl of Argyll. Needless to say he was not amused. A message arrived from the bereaved Maclean indicating that his wife had had an accident and had drowned. In typical Campbell subtlety, the Earl sent back word to Duart that the lady's body had in fact been found, and suggested that Maclean came with a coffin so that she could be buried at her old home. Lachlan Cattanach duly arrived with the coffin, but at the funeral feast had the disconcerting experience of finding the corpse to be acting as hostess. Exactly what Maclean's reaction was has not been recorded, but the Campbells emphasised their point a short time later when another brother of the lady, the Thane of Cawdor, caught up with Maclean when both happened to be in Edinburgh, and stabbed him to death in his bed.

One last brief episode. At the Battle of Inverkeithing in 1651, 800 of the Clan Gillean were among the Scots army facing Cromwell's Ironsides, and losing. Of these only 40 got back to Mull. Their Chief, Hector Roy, fell early, and one after another seven of his chieftains stepped forward to take his place and die over his body, each shouting 'Another for Hector!'

That was also the clan spirit.

Duchray Castle and
Two Commonwealths

Tucked in among the wooded foothills of the Trossachs mountains three miles west of Aberfoyle, Duchray is a little-known castle of modest size but of especially interesting history. Its appearance, however, is not improved by presumably Victorian attempts to increase its romantic impact by giving it arched Gothic-type windows. But it is still attractive and its setting very fine.

Like much of the land hereabouts, Duchray came to

the Grahams, as successors to the old Celtic earldom of Menteith. There was an earlier stronghold than this, on the edge of the Duchray Water's ravine, with parts of its thick walling incorporated in the present building. This seems to date from the second half of the 16th century, and is fairly typical, with circular stair-tower, an angle-turret and a curtain-walled court-yard, part of which still remains, again 'Gothicised'. The roof has been somewhat reduced in height. It was almost certainly built either by John Graham of Downance, a cadet of the Earls of Menteith, who bought the property in 1569, or by his son William.

That the Grahams required a fortified house here, in these quiet foothills, is not to be wondered at, for Duchray is on the very verge of the wild MacGregor country, the last jealously-guarded toehold of all the vast territories they once controlled. It lies a mere dozen miles, as the crow flies or the MacGregors marched, from Glengyle, their last chiefly residence, and about the same from Inversnaid on Loch Lomondside, Rob Roy's own lairdship. Nevertheless, although there must have been many occasions when the Grahams were glad of their stout walls to preserve them from the MacGregor's attentions, on both occasions recorded hereafter the Clan Alpin and the Grahams were in fact acting in concert.

Rob Roy himself once had an adventure here. He was visiting Duchray for purposes unspecified when a troop of Redcoats searching for him arrived at the castle. The two Graham sisters in residence did not lose their heads, however; and while one of them, considered to be somewhat simple, kept the officers engaged in talk at the main door, the other managed to smuggle Rob Roy out by a postern to the ravine below, down which he made his escape. I feel sure that Duchray's cattle must have been safer thereafter, without payment of 'mail'.

Strangely, on an earlier occasion, this small and remote fortalice was the headquarters of the Earl of Glencairn, in the only victorious attempt to resist the might of Oliver

Cromwell's Commonwealth troops. Victorious in that Glencairn's force beat Colonel Reid and his Ironsides at the small Battle of the Pass of Aberfoyle, in the cause of Charles II. Both Graham of Duchray and the MacGregors under Glengyle took vigorous part. Although this little triumph did not save Scotland from Cromwell, it helped to keep hope alive. Graham continued to assist Glencairn thereafter, on the King's behalf, and suffered accordingly. But Charles does not seem to have been any more grateful than he had been towards the great Montrose, for it was not until the accession of his brother, James VII and II, that the Scots Treasury were authorised to pay the Laird of Duchray the princely sum of £100 sterling in consideration of his loyalty and his losses.

Even after the Restoration Duchray seems to have been a magnet for excitements, for there took place a very odd affray, in 1671, when, coming from a christening-party of all things, Graham of Duchray and his people were ambushed on the old Bridge of Aberfoyle by the followers of the Earl of Airth, formerly Menteith, also Grahams. Just what this was all about I have never managed to discover. However, Duchray seems to have survived intact.

Still more odd is the following story. The Reverend Robert Kirk, a near relation of Graham of Duchray, the parish minister of Aberfoyle, was renowned for his belief in and alleged association with fairies, and wrote convincingly about them. It is recorded that, walking one day on the little hillock near the manse, whereon is a stone-circle, it being reputedly a fairy-mound, the minister sank to the ground unconscious, and was taken for dead. He did not revive, and his death being declared, his funeral followed in due and sad course. But shortly thereafter, he appeared to a relation, wearing the dress he had used on his walk, not funeral clothes, and told the alarmed individual that he was to go to Duchray and tell the laird that he was not dead, only had fallen into a swoon on meeting with some fairies and had been carried off to Fairyland. He was also to tell Laird Graham that when he and the others were assembled at the christening of his child — he had left a very pregnant wife — he would reappear to them all in the room. The laird was to pick up and throw a table knife over the reverend's head, whereupon he would be restored to human society.

The relative, perhaps deciding that he had dreamed all this, omitted to deliver this unusual message, whereupon Mr Kirk had to appear to him a second time. Thereafter he duly informed Duchray. Alas, at the christening-feast, as they were all sitting at table, the parish minister duly entered the room, but the laird was so overcome by the sight that he entirely forgot to throw the knife, and Mr Kirk passed out through another door and has never been seen since.

This account is given in the Notes to Walter Scott's *Rob Roy*; and at the time it was written was implicitly believed by the local folk.

It was, in fact, three years later before Mr Kirk's executors sufficiently satisfied that he was truly gone, were to publish his quite well-known work on the supernatural entitled *The Secret Commonwealth*.

Dundarave Castle and the Changeling

Picturesquely situated on a little headland on the north shore of Loch Fyne, the longest sea-loch in Scotland, some four miles north-west of Inveraray, and visible from the main A93 highway, this is a very typical late 16th century fortalice, with an untypical story. Once ruinous, it was handsomely restored in 1911 by the famous architect Sir Robert Lorimer. It is now a tall L-shaped building of five storeys, with stair-tower, angle-turrets and many shot-holes. It was the principal seat of the Chiefs of MacNaughton, descended from one Nachton Mhor, who flourished in the 10th century. Originally they were Thanes of Tayside, but by the time this castle was built, to replace one at the foot of nearby Glen Shira, their lands had been largely taken over by the Campbells, like those of the MacGregors; now they were living under the shadow, as it were, of their so powerful and acquisitive neighbours.

Dundarave features as *Castle Doom* in that novel by Neil Munro.

Donald MacNaughton of the Ilk took the side of MacDougal of Lorn and the Comyns against Robert the Bruce during the Wars of Independence; but after the hero-king's defeat at the Battle of Methven in 1306, when Bruce and the other survivors were ambushed by the MacDougals at Dalrigh, near Tyndrum, it is recorded that the extraordinary courage and ability shown by

Bruce who, in that narrow pass slew several of his attackers with his own hand, so impressed MacNaughton that he changed sides thereafter, and thenceforth became one of the hunted king's firmest supporters.

A descendant, Sir Alexander MacNaughton was knighted by James IV, and died with him on the fatal field of Flodden, like so many others.

But the castle did not survive with the MacNaughtons — not with the neighbours they had on Loch Fyne-side, and who had various methods of acquiring lands. The last of the MacNaughtons of Dundarave, around 1700, was engaged to wed the younger daughter of Sir James Campbell of Ardkinglas, just across Loch Fyne. Whether or not the wedding celebrations were too much for the bridegroom, he woke up next morning to find himself in bed with the wrong daughter, the elder one — his new father-in-law having his own reasons for the substitution. Preferring the other, however, MacNaughton fled with his chosen bride to Ireland — and thereafter the wily Campbell reigned at Dundarave. Thus sank the family, to the extent that the laird's brother had to take the humble position of collector of customs at the little port of Anstruther in Fife.

The MacNaughtons, as a clan, remained loyal to the House of Stewart, one supporting Bonnie Dundee at Killiecrankie, and another being one of Queen Anne's guards killed at Vigo in 1702. The Chief of the Culdares branch, who had been pardoned for his part in the 1715 Rising, is linked with a touching story. Because he had been pardoned, he did not actively join Prince Charlie in 1745 — but instead sent him a notably fine charger to ride on into England. The MacNaughton servant who conveyed the horse to the prince was however captured, and along with so many others was tried for treason at Carlisle. He pointed out that he had done no fighting, only brought the horse to the prince as a present. He was offered a pardon and his life if he would reveal the name of the sender of the gift. This, with indignation, the clans-

man refused to do, asking if his captors could suppose him to be such a villain, and declaring that his life was nothing to that of his master. So he was hanged.

It is perhaps significant that over the door of Dundarave Castle, with the date 1596, is this inscription: BEHALD THE END, BE NOCHT VYSER NOR THE HIEST.

Dunnottar Castle and the Honours of Scotland

O n surely one of the most dramatic sites for a castle in all Scotland, so full of imposing defensive situations as it is, Dunnottar was a major stronghold — and the surviving remains are still major and spectacular — set on their isolated rock-top above the waves of a savage coastline a couple miles south of Stonehaven, in The Mearns. During the Pictish period indeed this was the site of the ancient capital of The Mearns; but in the 14th century Sir William Keith, Great Marischal of Scotland, chose to build his fortalice here — thereby provoking the wrath of the Vatican, for he removed an early church to do so. He was actually excommunicated by the then Pope, but managed to gain remission by building another church in what must surely have been a more convenient position.

The castle was added to as time went on and the Keiths grew in power and dignity, to become Earls Marischal, and the stronghold became almost like a clifftop village, with a number of detached buildings, its extensions from the original L-shaped keep including retainers' barracks, a chapel, priest's house, stables, even a graveyard. How they got the horses up to the said stables exercises the imagination! Highiy interesting, in more respects than one, is the entrance gatehouse, at the head of a steep climbing track, this defended by no fewer than three tiers of defensive walls with splayed gun-loops; and the eventual arched gateway 35 feet high crowned with a parapet, and of course, using the natural rock for added security and threat. Oddly, there was another access, by means of a cavelike tunnel and steps cut in the interior of the rock itself, which could be blocked with the utmost ease by the defenders.

Donnottar had a stirring history which can only be hinted at here. Wallace captured it during the Wars of Independence. Edward III did likewise, but it fell again to Sir Andrew Moray, who became Regent of Scotland. The fifth Earl Marischal, who founded Marischal College at Aberdeen, erected most of the extensions. Montrose besieged the castle but lacking siege artillery, could only burn much of the Marischal's surrounding property as warning. Charles II was entertained here by the ninth Earl in 1650, and the following year it was selected as the strongest place in the kingdom to deposit the Scottish regalia of crown, orb, sceptres and sword-of-state, to preserve all from Cromwell's invading army. This episode represents probably Dunnottar's most renowned story.

The Cromwellian General Lambert came to besiege

the castle, and in time, with starvation facing the garrison, it was decided that somehow the Honours of Scotland should be smuggled out before the place fell. This was contrived in ingenious fashion. The minister of the nearby Kinneff parish, the Reverend James Grainger, and his brave wife, now played the undying role in history. Christian Grainger was friendly with the wife of George Ogilvy of Barras the Earl Marischal's lieutenant-governor of Dunnottar, and one day she presented herself, on horseback and with a maid, before Major-General Morgan, whom Lambert had left to conduct the siege, requesting his permission to visit Mrs Ogilvy — since, she said, she was sure that English gentlemen did not make war on women. The General, even a Puritan one, but no doubt a Welshman, evidently could not resist that and she was granted admission. Thereafter, with Mrs Ogilvy's aid, she pushed Scotland's crown up under her skirts and wrapped the orb and sceptres in lint to look like a distaff, and with her servant carrying these, made her presumably very awkward way out and down. It is said that Morgan, quite dazzled by Mrs Grainger's charms, for she must have looked a great deal more pregnant than when she arrived, actually and gallantly aided the lady up on to her horse. At any rate, she got the regalia safely back to Kinneff, where she and her husband put it all under their box-bed; but later, for security's sake, buried it beneath the pulpit of the church one night — the subject of a famous and dramatic painting. In due course, at the Restoration, the precious relics were handed over to King Charles.

The rewards for this piece of romantic initiative were oddly out-of-proportion. The Graingers were granted 2,000 merks — quite a sum for a country minister, no doubt, but paltry for the service rendered. Ogilvy was created a baronet, so that his wife became Lady Ogilvy; and of all things, Sir John Keith, brother of the Earl Marischal, whose only connection with the affair was that he had accepted custody of the Honours in the first place, but had smuggled himself out of the castle early in the siege to go for aid, and was captured and imprisoned — he was created Earl of Kintore, with a state pension. Such is the way of the world.

Not so long afterwards Dunnottar was shamefully used as a state prison by the royalist side, and here 167 men and women were barbarously confined in one crowded cell, still known as the Whigs' Vault. Twenty five made a desperate attempt to escape down the beetling cliffs, and two fell to their deaths. The others, recaptured were terribly tortured by the governor, Keith of Whiterigs — all in the name of religion. Sir Walter Scott visiting here in 1793 and seeing the memorial being cleaned, gained thereby the idea for his *Old Mortality*.

Fairburn Tower and
the Brahan Seer

The great clan of Mackenzie, the Sons of Kenneth, were at one time as all-powerful in Ross, Easter and Wester, as were the Campbells in Argyll — which is saying something. They started out on the western seaboard and islands, of course, with their Chiefs making Kintail, on the mainland opposite Skye, their main seat. But as the ancient earldom of Ross, largely based on Easter Ross, went down, so the Mackenzies rose and took over, spreading ever eastwards to those more fertile lands, until presently there was scarcely an estate or barony on all the eastern seaboard and the Black Isle of Cromarty which did not have a Mackenzie laird. The Chiefs themselves, who had become first Lords Mackenzie of Kintail, and then, at the twelfth, Earls of Seaforth, moved over to Braham Castle near Dingwall. And a cadet line, Mackenzie of Tarbat, near Nigg Bay, became Earls of Cromartie. As well as these, there were many baronetcies and innumerable influential lairdships — Gairloch, Coul, Scotwell, Redcastle, Kilcoy, Avoch, Kinkell, Ardloch and others. Amongst these, one of the richest and most powerful was Fairburn. And in the second half of the 17th century, Roderick, fifth of Fairburn, was reputed to be the richest laird in Ross.

His castle, now a ruin, still stands high on a long ridge between the straths of Orrin and Conon, five miles northwest of Muir of Ord, within the large estate of the present more modern mansion. It is a lofty and impressive tower, complete to the wallhead but long roofless, looking a fairly typical fortalice of the late 16th century. But in fact it dates from two periods, the massive oblong keep with thick walling, to which in the early 17th century was added a tall and fairly slender stair-tower, as a wing, to provide more convenient access to the upper stories — and this stair-tower plays a significant part in Fairburn's tale.

The tradition concerns the Brahan Seer. This famous 17th-century character was almost as renowned as a soothsayer in the North of Scotland as was Thomas the Rhymer in the South four centuries earlier. Unlike True Thomas, the Brahan Seer came to a very unpleasant end, being enclosed in a spiked barrel and rolled down a hill,

according to local story, before being burned. This on account of the spite of a Countess of Seaforth, or so tradition avers.

The Fairburn connection went thus. The seer one day came upon a group of the Mackenzie lairds who, out hunting, had all but ridden down a young woman gathering herbs on Fairburn Muir, and balked of their deer, were making sport of the girl. Kenneth the seer, coming to her rescue, rebuked them boldly, and in the subsequent angry exchange, delivered some dire predictions as to the lairds' and their houses' future. Roderick Mackenzie of Fairburn, on whose lands they were hunting, was the most hot and threatening, demanding to know who was this insolent individual who dared to counter a baron on his own land, and threatening what he would do to him — after all, he held the power of pit and gallows there.

'Be not so quick to speak ill words, Fairburn,' the sooth-sayer advised. 'For the day is coming when there will be no Mackenzies at Fairburn, and your line will vanish from the face of this earth. Your fine castle will stand empty and abandoned, and a cow will give birth to its calf in the topmost watch-chamber of your tower!'

He was laughed to scorn, of course, at voicing such fantasies, and the other lairds joined in — Redcastle, Kilcoy, Avoch. Kenneth pointed at each, one after the other. Redcastle, he declared who could not keep his seed to himself, would have a female half-wit born among his descendants in each generation. Kilcoy's castle would house only one filthy old man, shunned by all, living in what was almost a ruin. And Avoch — who was the famous Bluidy Mackenzie, Sir George Mackenzie of Rosehaugh, Lord Advocate — would have his lands lost to his family and into the hands of the common fishermen of Avoch. High-powered cursing for the up-and-coming Clan Kenneth.

Well, all these prophesies, in course of time, were fulfilled. This is not the place to go into details as to these last three. But as to Fairburn, the line came to an end in 1850, with the death, unmarried, of General Sir Alexander Mackenzie. Nothing so very extraordinary about that. But for some years before this the tower had ceased to be the family seat, replaced by the later mansion. Nothing unusual about that either. The local tenant-farmer used the old castle to store his hay; and, a year after the laird's death, somehow a cow in calf found its way in at the narrow doorway. Following a trail of hay, it worked its way up the fairly wide circular stair of the 17th-century tower — something it could by no means have done in the earlier turnpike within the thickness of the keep walling — until it got right to the top and into the caphouse. And there, being unable to find its way down again, it stayed, and duly produced its calf. So it had to remain for some time — long enough for the news of this extraordinary happening to get bruited abroad, and even for one of the newly formed railway's special trains to be run from Inverness to Muir of Ord to enable interested citizens to come and see the wonder of the Brahan Seer's prophesy fulfilled. That stair-tower is six storeys high, so the sight was worth coming to inspect.

Finavon Castle
and the Tiger

A ll that remains of Finavon Castle today is a very
lofty square tower, 86ft high, standing isolated in
the grounds of a more modern mansion, five
miles north of Forfar in Angus. For long this was almost
the hub and centre of all Angus, the seat of its greatest
lords, the premier Earls of all Scotland, the Lindsay Earls
of Crawford. Sufficient has happened here to fill volumes. The line still continues, but not in Finavon Castle.

To even hint at this castle's story demands major and
galling selection. It was built in the 15th century,
although almost certainly there was an earlier stronghold
on the site, where the Lemno Burn joins the South Esk. Of
the long line of the Crawford Earls — the present one is
the 29th — many have undoubtedly been excellent characters. But it is, of course, usually the villains who get the
publicity and from whom stem the stories, a sad com-
mentary on human nature. Let us start, at least, with the
heroic first Earl, David, so created in 1398, having married the daughter of Robert II, Bruce's grandson. As Sir
David Lindsay he was the finest tournament-jouster of
his day, and in the presence of the English King and
Queen in 1390 not only unhorsed the English champion,
the Lord Welles, but seemed to suffer no shock in his own
saddle, so that the crowd yelled that he was somehow
fastened on. To prove otherwise he actually vaulted to
the ground and then back into the saddle, an extraordi-

nary feat of strength in massive plate-armour. In the hand-to-hand contest on foot which followed, he performed the astonishing manoeuvre of hoisting the unfortunate Welles up on the point of his dagger and then throwing him to the ground.

His grandson, another David, third Earl, seems to have been of a comparatively peaceable nature, for he was killed in 1445 while trying to stop the Battle of Arbroath between the Lindsays on one side and the Ogilvys of Auchterhouse and Inverquharity on the other, with Huntly-Gordon support. He did not actually die on the field, but was brought back to Finavon — oddly, along with his wounded brother-in-law, who was in fact Ogilvy of Inverquharity, fighting on the other side. And so distraught was the Countess of Crawford, when her husband breathed his last, that she hurried through to the room where her brother lay and smothered him with a pillow.

Presumably their son and heir, Alexander, fourth Earl, inherited his mother's nature rather than his father's, for this was the ferocious Tiger Earl, or Earl Beardie, about whom there are grim stories galore. He it was who hanged a minstrel from iron hooks at the top of the tower for unspecified reasons; but before he died the minstrel prophesied that he, and the Earl of Douglas, his master's ally, would suffer resounding defeat at Brechin. It perhaps should be mentioned that this was in James II's reign when the King had a deadly hatred of the Douglases. The Earl of Crawford, the Earl of Douglas and the Lord of the Isles, all linked by marriage to the crown, entered into a treasonable 'band' to partition the kingdom between them. Anyway, they were soundly defeated at the Battle of Brechin in 1452, as the minstrel foretold; and the Tiger Earl, on his return to Finavon, is recorded as declaring that he would gladly pass seven years in hell to have gained the victory. This is interesting in view of his latter activities.

Amongst these was his shameful killing of a

messenger-boy, from Careston, a neighbouring estate, who cut a branch from the Covin Tree of Finavon, allegedly for a walking-stick. For this the Earl hanged Jockie Barefoot on another branch of the said tree that grew in the courtyard, first having cut out his tongue. The local tradition had it that Jockie still runs between Finavon and Careston Castles trying to deliver his message and lacking a tongue to do it.

When King James heard of this and other crimes, he swore that he would bring down the Tiger and, as he put it, make the highest stone of Finavon the lowest.

However, either the Earl was too strong for the monarch or else promised good behaviour, for he won remission and James relented, after receiving sumptuous entertainment at Finavon. However, to fulfil his vow, he climbed to the top of the tower where he duly pushed over a block of masonry from the parapet to the ground 86 feet below. This stone was long kept chained to the tower-foot — but now there are too many other fallen stones to identify this one.

It was this fourth Earl, of course, who, playing cards in the secret room of Glamis Castle, not far away, and losing so badly against the first Lord Glamis, was advised to give up for the night, answered 'Never — even until the Day of Judgment!' Whereupon the Devil himself joined in, and the room and occupants vanished — or so they say — even although its window remains visible on the outer walling.

The fifth Earl, another David, son of the Tiger, was possibly the most distinguished of the line, becoming Keeper of Berwick, Lord High Admiral of Scotland, Lord Chamberlain and High Justiciar. He was created Duke of Montrose in 1489, but his successors did not claim the dukedom on his death, preferring to be known as Earls of Crawford. These did not all live up to his fame, it is to be feared. His son, the sixth Earl, was accused, with his sister-in-law, of murdering his brother, the Master of Crawford; but the enquiry into this crime was interrupted by the Battle of Flodden, at which the Earl fell, with so many others. He was succeeded by his uncle who only lived for four more years, and had a son David, eighth Earl, who was for 13 weeks imprisoned in Finavon's dungeon by his own son, 'The Wicked Master' — who 11 years later was stabbed to death by a Dundee cobbler for snatching from him a tankard of ale.

The 10th Earl married Margaret, daughter of Cardinal David Beaton, at Finavon and the nuptials were celebrated with a munificence hitherto unknown.

But in 1629 Finavon was sold by the 14th Earl, and its

decay began. Perhaps we should all have an interest in its ultimate fate, for Thomas the Rhymer made this prophesy:

'When Finhaven Castle rins to sand,
The warld's end is near at hand'.

Gilnockie Tower and Johnnie

Most folk will have heard, at least, of the Border ballad of Johnnie Armstrong — and a spirited and proud sad tale it is. But probably comparatively few know of his home in the castle which he built in Upper Eskdale — for the Armstrongs are renowned as a Liddesdale clan from the Debateable Lands, well to the east and actually on the Borderline. But Johnnie was Armstrong of Gilnockie; and Gilnockie Tower stands on the Esk, in Canonbie parish about four miles south of Langholm. Johnnie, younger brother of Christopher Armstrong of Mangerton, in Liddesdale, Chief of the clan, built it about 1518.

There has been some confusion about this castle and its name. Many maps show it as Hollows Tower — a corruption of Holehouse — less than half a mile north of the present Hollows Bridge which carries the A7 across the Esk, with a green mound at the roadside south of the bridge marked as the site of Gilnockie Tower. This is a mistake, and proven so, despite errors dating from the New Statistical Account of 1836. The site near the bridge was probably that of an ancient earthen-ramparted Pictish fort or dun, and no traces of masonry have been found there. Whereas the building to the north, very obvious from the main road, is a typical square Border peel-tower of the 16th century, massive-walled, of four storeys below a corbelled parapet and wall-walk, with a garret storey above, the crow-stepped gable surmounted by a stone beacon for a watch-fire. All would formerly be surrounded by a high barmekin or curtain-wall, the peel or paling of the name.

This fine tower was a roofless ruin until recently, although otherwise well-preserved. Now happily, it has been restored by a descendant of the Armstrongs and is once again a home.

Johnnie of Gilnockie is the best-known of all the Armstrong chieftains, and deservedly so, one of the most colourful and successful characters ever to set the Borders by the ears — which is saying something. His chiefly brother seems to have been a much less dramatic individual and soon Johimie was leading that fierce and unruly clan with ever increasing audacity. He seems to have preceded Rob Roy MacGregor in bringing to a fine art the protection racket; and his reiving and raiding exploits, his sallies over the Border, his tussles with both the English and Scots Wardens of the Marches, his feats of personal daring, and so on, would fill a book. Walter Scott went into raptures over him. Whenever tales of the Borderland are told, Johnnie Armstrong's name is apt to crop up.

Johnnie, you see, had a flair for more than just the usual reiving and cattle-stealing, and made his presence felt far and wide, and deep into England. He adopted a great gallantry towards the ladies, at least the Scots ladies:

> ' ... *never a Scots wyfe could have said,*
> *That e'er I skaithed her a puir flee.'*

He became something of a king in the West March, boasting that he never rode abroad with a tail of less than 36 gentlemen of his own name, landed men not just mosstroopers. All this did not please some of his neighbours, needless to say, and many were the complaints to the King of Scots, especially from Henry VIII of England. At length young James V, to be father of Mary Queen of Scots but at this time only 17 years old, decided that something drastic would have to be done about Johnnie Armstrong. A typical armed expedition would not serve, however, for it could not be moved south without warning; and when warned, Johnnie could reputedly muster as many as 2000 mounted mosstroopers, and in difficult campaigning country. So James resorted to guile and sent a fair invitation for Johnnie to meet him, on a hunting trip, at Caerlanrig Chapel, near Teviothead, in a 'luving letter' as the ballad puts it. Johnnie elected to accede to his liege-lord's request, and duly arrived with his 36 gentlemen, all clad in their best, more finely turned out than the monarch's court. 'What lacks this knave that a King should have?' young James Stewart demanded hotly, at the sight; and beat about the bush no longer, commanding that Johnnie and his 36 should be strung up from convenient trees there and then. The Armstrong was too proud to plead for his life; but he did bargain.

His offerings, however, were such as only to make matters worse, like terms for a treaty between two equal princes. He offered to provide the King with 40 armed and horsed gentlemen to attend him at all times, at his own expense — apart from the squadrons of mosstroopers he could always raise. He offered 24 milk-white horses and as much good English gold as four of them could carry. He offered the produce of 24 meal-mills annually. He offered to bring the King of Scots any Englishmen he liked to name, be he duke, earl or baron, alive or dead, by any given day. And finally he offered a rent on every property between where they stood and the city of Newcastle.

When all this, not unnaturally, made James only the more anxious to dispose of such a dangerous object, John nie made his famous valedictory speech: 'It was folly to seek grace at Your Grace's graceless face; but had I known it I should have lived long upon the Borders in despite of King Harry and you both; for I know that King Harry would downweigh my best horse with gold to hear that I were condemned to die this day.'

And so the Armstrongs were hanged. The Borderers declare that the trees which bore them withered away thereafter at the manifest injustice of the deed; certainly there are none at Caerlanrig now. The renowned Sir David Lindsay of the Mount, author of *The Thrie Estates*, wrote, putting the words into the mouth of a pardoner, a dealer in relics:

'The cordis, baith grit and lang,
Qhuilk hangit Johnie Armstrang,
Of gude hemp, soft and sound,
Gude haly people, I stand ford,
Wha'evir beis hangit in this cord,
Neidis never to be drowned!'

It is a good to think that there are Armstrongs again in Gilnockie; but where are the Stewarts?

Castle Girnigoe and
Sinclair's Law

Perched dizzily on an almost detached rock promontory jutting into the Pentland Firth, about three miles north of Wick, in Caithness, this castle is unusual in more than its scarcely believable story; for there are in fact two distinct fortalices here, the late 15th-century Girnigoe itself and, detached across a narrow, ravine-like gap in the cliff, Sinclair Castle, of the early 17th century. Why the Sinclairs chose to do it this way, instead of building a larger house elsewhere, if needing more room, is a matter for conjecture. Both are now ruinous, the later building much more so than the more massively built Girnigoe.

The story starts in 1455 when James III compelled William St. Clair, third Earl of Orkney of 'the lordly line of high St. Clair', to resign his earldom and Orkney domains, which he had held of the King of Denmark, on these being ceded to Scotland as security for the unpaid dowry of the Danish Princess Margaret whom James had married. St. Clair was created Earl of Caithness instead and given large lands on the mainland. His second son succeeded him and probably built Girnigoe as his main seat. In which case he must have been a man of strange, wild tastes.

It is a tall, gaunt fang of a building, approximately E-shaped to follow the odd contours of the rocky constricted site, with the different parts of the castle at

different base levels — and much scope for semi-subterranean vaults and dungeons. It can never have been a comfortable place. Indeed comfort is perhaps the last impression given by Girnigoe, a stark and savage hold on a stark and savage seaboard — which makes one wonder all the more why the later castle was erected here alongside.

And some of the ongoings here were quite as savage as were the looks of the place; in fact few Scots castles can have had such a history of sheer ferocity. Herein, for instance, George, fourth Earl of Caithness, imprisoned his eldest son and heir, John, Master of Caithness, in one of the many semi-subterranean cells for seven long years, allegedly on suspicion of uprising against him but really because he was displeased by John's 'lenity towards the townfolk of Dornoch'. This is strange, since in 1570, six years earlier, the said John had burned Dornoch Cathedral and plundered the town. Be that as it may, the Earl having kept his son all these years in the cell, grew impatient that he survived, and had him fed 'on a large mess of salt beef, and then, withholding all drink from him, left him to die of raging thirst', the wretched victim having first gone mad.

This unnatural father was Justiciar of Caithness, as well as Earl, so one can guess the sort of justice Caithness received. Incidentally he was a keen supporter of Mary Queen of Scots and indeed sat as chairman of the jury which acquitted Bothwell of Darnley's murder. As it happened, the said son John was married to Bothwell's sister.

There seems to have been something far wrong with these early Sinclair Earls. The imprisoned John had a son George, who succeeded his grandfather as fifth Earl, and seems to have inherited the family violence. He promptly had the two Sinclairs who had been his father's gaolers murdered, which perhaps was reasonable by the standards of the day — at least, in 1584, he received a remission from the Privy Council, under the Great Seal, for this act. He quarrelled incessantly with the neighbouring Earl of Sutherland and wild were the excitements, until he was bound over to keep the peace on pain of outlawry — although whether outlawry could have been enforced on him in Caithness is doubtful. At any rate he changed his activities somewhat, to keep himself amused. It is recorded that when servants of the new Earl of Orkney, son of one of Queen Mary's half-brothers, were driven ashore near Girnigoe in a storm, he made them drunk, then had one side of their hair and beards shaved off, and sent them back into the storm. He set up a mint to forge false coin at Girnigoe — we have the forger's name, Arthur Smith — and circulated this money throughout the North of Scotland. Oddly, this character was then made a Commissioner of the Peace, and as such handed over to

James VI and I a guest who was staying with him at Girnigoe. Then he led an armed expedition to Orkney to put down a rebellion by the aforementioned Earl of Orkney, Patrick Stewart — for which service King James summoned him to London and gave him a pension of 1,000 crowns a year. He could not keep up this turn towards virtue, however, and directed his attentions on the tenants of the Lord Forbes who had recently acquired lands in Caithness, presumably against the Earl's wishes. He got the Clan Gunn people to burn the Forbes corn and let it be known that this had been done by the Mackays. When the Mackays brought witnesses to the Commissioner of the Peace to prove that they were innocent, he had the witnesses drowned. For this he had his thousand-crown pension stopped, and in 1643 he died at a great age, bankrupt, to be succeeded by his great-grandson.

This unfortunate young man had to cope not only with his great-grandfather's debts but with Oliver Cromwell, who sent an expedition to take Girnigoe, and planted therein a garrison of 70 foot and 15 horse. He married a daughter of the Marquis of Argyll, Montrose's great enemy — thereby ensuring much trouble for himself and Girnigoe — for when he died without issue in 1676, his widow promptly married her own kinsman, Sir John Campbell of Glenorchy, one of his great-grandfather's creditors, who thereupon claimed the earldom of Caithness in her right and on account of his debt; and in 1679 led an army to besiege Castle Girnigoe, to get by force what seemed to be denied him by law. He defeated the Sinclairs at Wick, and that seems to have been the end of Girnigoe's hectic story. It is perhaps interesting to note that the well-known song, *The Campbells are Coming*, was first written to celebrate this event, and its connection with the Relief of Lucknow by Sir Colin Campbell, was merely a 'replay'.

Harthill Castle and
the Awkward Laird

Aberdeenshire is richly endowed with castles, many of them splendid and storied. But few, surely are more storied and now more splendid, than Harthill at the back o' Bennachie. It was not always so, admittedly, for Harthill was a ruin until recently, when a far-seeing American lady, after a considerable search, found and restored it as one of the most handsome homes in the North.

Harthill is tall, towered and turreted, standing below the green northern skirts of Bennachie, that dramatic, isolated mountain of Central Aberdeenshire, not far from Oyne, in the fair valley of the Urie. Amongst other features it is notable in retaining its gabled gatehouse, or part of it, the fortified entrance to the walled courtyard, which always surrounded these fortalices but which was usually swept away when defence was considered to be no longer necessary. Here a handsome example, formerly heraldically decorated, it has survived, although no attempt has been made to restore it.

Harthill's story is as dramatic as its appearance, although sometimes perhaps less dignified. Like not a few others in the Urie and Don valleys this was a Leith strong hold, a family a little less numerous but no less vigorous than the Gordons and Forbeses. Without these three clans Aberdeenshire's history would have been pale indeed. There presumably was an earlier castle at

Harthill, for the first Leith thereof had a charter from James V in 1531; whereas the present house dates from the first half of the succeeding century, allegedly built by Patrick Leith, a cadet of Leithhall, in 1638 — but by its architectural details appearing somewhat to pre-date that. Young Harthill was noted for his bravery and leadership in the army of the great Montrose, fighting for King Charles against the Covenanter forces. He was captured by General Middleton in 1647 and executed by beheading, at the age of 25.

Harthill was inherited by his brother John, who was also a royalist of a sort, but of a very different temperament. It is recorded that once, entering the famous mother-church of Aberdeen, St. Nicholas, during mid-service, he insisted on taking the Provost's seat. This was certainly by no mistake, for being the official place of worship for the citizens it boasts a notable Provost's and Magistrates' Gallery, canopied by a magnificent baldachino. Harthill was offered another seat, and when he refused it, was remonstrated with, all this while the service continued. He drew his sword and swore:

'By God's wounds, I'll sit beside the Provost and in no other place!'

This was too much, even from a Leith laird, and Harthill was arrested and jailed. On trial thereafter he asserted that the Provost was 'ane doittit cock and ane ass', and snatching the complaint from the clerk of court, he tore it up. Not only that, but picking up the inkhorn and pen-holder from the dock, he cast it in the unfortunate clerk's face and thereby 'hurt and wounded him in two several parts to the great effusion of blood'.

Not content even with this show of lairdly independ ence, while new legal proceedings were under way, Harthill set the jail on fire, somehow managed to arm sundry other prisoners, took over the burning premises and fired on the populace. Eventually this awkward customer was overcome, and presumably confined within more secure walls somewhere, for he was not released until nine months later when Montrose again gained mastery over Scotland for a while — so presumably he had done it all in the sacred name of King Charles. It was just as well that General Middleton was not commanding in Aberdeen at the time, or John would surely have followed his brother Patrick to the block.

We hear no more of this spirited character, but four generations later the last Leith laird of Harthill seems to have been something of the same type, for he is reported to have been on such ill terms with all his neighbours, that he decided on drastic action, set fire to Harthill and left Aberdeenshire and Scotland for good, in fact dying a pauper in London.

With this background I would think that the present owners would have some difficulty in living up to Harthill tradition.

Hawthornden Castle and the King's Caves

Because of its association with the famous 17th-century poet, 'the Scots Petrarch', Drummond of Hawthornden, this castle's repute and stories tend to be confined to that period and its literary anecdotes as, for instance in 1618-19 when Ben Jonson walked all the way on foot from London to visit Drummond here; and once at Hawthornden stayed for three weeks, by which time his host was thoroughiy tired of him; and how, in 1649, Drummond himself died here of a broken heart, allegedly, on learning of the execution of King Charles I. And so on. Which is a pity, for although these tales are interesting enough, Hawthornden has so much more to relate than that.

Its situation itself is sufficiently dramatic, perched like some eagle's nest on a high shelf of a cliff in the precipitous wooded valley of the Midlothian North Esk, a mile north-east of Roslin. Not only so but it is built above a positive honeycomb of caves in the soft red sandstone cliff, alleged to be artificial but which no doubt are in part natural. These ensured that this was a strategic and defensive site from very early times, probably Pictish; and in fact it is these caves which were responsible in large measure for Hawthornden's most stirring stories. They are reached from the castle-courtyard by a deep shaft and ladder and there is also a very deep draw-well for the water supply. The caves are linked by corridors cut in the rock and three of them bear royal names — the King's Gallery, the King's Bed-Chamber and the King's DiningRoom — the King in this case being Robert the Bruce, who, like Wallace before him, used Hawthornden in his long struggle against English domination. Indeed it was during the Wars of Independence that Hawthornden attained its greatest fame, although little of the present castle dates from so early. One of the caves is actually carved with stone nesting-boxes as a dovecote, with access to the cliff face. The pigeons would be a valuable source of fresh meat in any siege conditions, whatever the smell!

Oddly, despite all this emphasis on King Robert, there are few details about the hero-king's activities at Hawthornden. The most stirring of its stories date from the slightly later wars, after Bruce's death, when he was succeeded by his child-son David II, and the English renewed their assaults on Scotland. One of these occasions is referred to on a table set in the castle-walling by the then Bishop of Edinburgh, Dr. William Abernethy Drummond (1720-1809). It says: 'To the memory of Sir Lawrence Abernethy of Hawthornden, a brave and

gallant soldier, who in 1338 conquered Lord Douglas five times in one day, yet was taken prisoner before sunset'. I imagine that the good Bishop was not terribly well up on his history, for the said Sir Lawrence may have been brave but he was scarcely gallant, for he was at this time fighting on the English side, as he had done previously and then changed to Bruce's side when he saw who was winning. The 'Lord' Douglas referred to here is Sir William Douglas the Knight of Liddesdale. We all make mistakes sometimes.

However, I think that undoubtedly the most colourful and inspiring story of Hawthornden relates to that patriotic, courageous but unfortunate leader in these wars, Sir Alexander Ramsay of Dalwolsey, the original name for what is now Dalhousie, also in Midlothian. In the same year, 1338, the English under Salisbury laid siege to the castle of Dunbar, and in the absence of her lord, the Earl of Dunbar and March, the Countess, the famous Black Agnes of Dunbar, maintained an intrepid stand against the invaders for no less than five months, managing to receive supplies by sea. The English had to bring up a fleet to blockade the harbour and castle, and thereafter things looked black indeed for Black Agnes — so called for her dark good looks. Then Sir Alexander Ramsay came to her rescue. After hiding behind the Bass Rock, he sailed in a light vessel and stood in for Dunbar in the darkness managing to pass though the English line unobserved, to run his ship, laden with provisions and his own 40 stout men-at-arms to reinforce the garrison, right under the walls of Dunbar Castle on its cliff-site; thus enabling the defenders, whom he now joined, to resist for a further indefinite period. In disgust Salisbury broke off the siege.

But now the English invaders were after Ramsay, who was already a marked man from previous exploits, determined to hunt him down. He came here to Hawthornden with his 40 men, and they hid themselves in the caves, the secret of which was unknown to the enemy. Indeed it was small wonder that it was not known, for even now the only access to them is down the deep well-shaft of the castle water-supply, where a tunnel opens off. From here Sir Alexander sallied forth from time to time, careful always not to give away his hiding-place, and harassed the English not only locally and in Edinburgh but right down into Northumberland. So worried did the enemy become over this guerilla warfare that the Earl of Derby sent a herald out seeking to invite Sir Alexander to a three-day jousting contest, under safe-conduct, at Berwick-on-Tweed, a nice touch. Whether this was an entirely chivalrous gesture or a way of getting Ramsay's whereabouts pin-pointed, is a matter of debate. At any rate, Ramsay heard of and accepted the challenge and duly turned up at Berwick, where he managed to unseat and slay two English knights in single combat. Thereafter he contrived to get away and resumed his depredations over the Border, from his base at Hawthornden, on one occasion not only routing a large enemy convoy but capturing its leader, the Lord Robert Manners. But always he returned to his secret cave hideaway, below the castle.

It seems tragic that this paladin should have ended up being starved to death in Hermitage Castle by the so-called Flower of Chivalry, his old comrade-in-arms, Sir William Douglas of Liddesdale, as recounted in the following chapter.

Let us end this account on a more cheerful if less heroic note, reverting to the literary. This is the caustic comment by John Wolcot (Peter Pindar) on the visit here of the great Dr Johnson:

'Went to Hawthornden's fair scene by night,
Lest o'er a Scottish tree should lose his sight!'

Hermitage Castle and a Queen's Love

The very model and epitome of a great Border stronghold, despite its odd name — presumably it was built on the site of some Celtic saint's lonely sanctuary or hermitage — this great castle soars above the water of the same name in Liddesdale, up a remote side-valley of the West March some five miles north by east of Newcastleton. It was often the seat of the Wardens of the West March, although always a private fortalice, never a national fortress. Its story is on a par with its appearance.

The original castle seems to have been built by Sir Nicholas de Soulis, although the property appears to have belonged to the Comyns for a period previously. These were, of course, both Norman families introduced into Scotland by David I, after his long sojourn as a kind of hostage at the Norman court at Winchester; and Nicholas de Soulis was a Comyn supporter and became Lord of Liddesdale in the late 13th century. This was a most difficult area to control, of course, and these tough Norman soldiers were just the men to do it. Their methods were the reverse of gentle, needless to say, and Hermitage has seen much of cruelty and savagery. Indeed there is local tradition that Sir William de Soulis, son of Sir Nicholas, was boiled alive by his outraged Border vassals on Nine Stane Rig, a hill with a nine-stone stone-circle, to the east of the castle. This appears to be a

mistake, for Sir William, who rose against Robert the Bruce, died a prisoner in the royal fortress of Dumbarton, whereafter Bruce gave Hermitage to the more trustworthy Douglases. The victim of the boiling must have been another of the family.

Not that the Douglases proved so much more gentle. The famous Sir William Douglas, Knight of Liddesdale, was known as the Flower of Chivalry. However, that title could hardly survive his treatment of Sir Alexander Ramsay of Dalwolsey, or Dalhousie. Ramsay was a gallant soldier and during the unhappy reign of Bruce's son, David II, won special renown by his struggle against the English domination and his recapture of the great Roxburgh Castle from the Auld Enemy. For this service he was made Sheriff of Teviotdale, an office hitherto held by Sir William Douglas of Liddesdale. To show his displeasure, Douglas managed to capture Ramsay and confined him in a cell at Hermitage, without food or water. It is recorded that the unfortunate man managed to survive for 17 days by grubbing on the floor for grains of corn which had dropped down through the floor-boards from a granary above.

Grim as this deed was, it does not seem to have been

the one which was responsible for the former Flower of Chivalry's end. This was occasioned by a particularly unpleasant secret negotiation with Edward III of England, whereby he promised Edward's armies access into Scotland at any time through the West March and his lands, on condition that Liddesdale remained his if the Plantagenet King achieved his aim of becoming Lord Paramount of Scotland. Douglas's own kinsman, the first Earl of Douglas, got to hear of this, and being more loyal, captured the Knight of Liddesdale while hunting in Ettrick Forest and slew him there and then.

This was not the last of Douglas treacheries, by any means, for another of them, Archibald-Bell-the-Cat, Earl of Angus, on his way back to Hermitage from a surreptitious and treasonable visit in the reign of James III, to Henry VII of England, was met by the Lord Lyon King of Arms, with a large force, and taken instead to his castle of Tantallon in Lothian and immured there — although only for a short time, for the Douglases were always too strong for a weak monarch.

However, James IV was anything but weak, and he made the Earl of Angus exchange Hermitage for Bothwell Castle in Lanarkshire — where he presumably thought that he could do less harm than on the sensitive Borders with England — and installed the Hepburn Earl of Bothwell at Hermitage in his place. And of course it is in the Bothwell period that Hermitage's most famous incident took place, in the reign of this James's granddaughter, Mary.

As we all know, Mary Queen of Scots fell in love with James Hepburn, fourth Earl of Bothwell, who like his predecessors at Hermitage was Warden of the Marches. In October 1566 he was wounded by one of the Border reivers called Little Jock Elliot of Park, was carried back to Hermitage where he lay seriously sick. The Queen at this time was holding justice-ayres at Jedburgh, almost 30 miles to the east across the spine of the land. When she heard of Bothwell's trouble, she, with a party of her nobles, set out to ride across the hills to Hermitage as soon as she could get away from her justice-sittings. There she remained two hours at Bothwell's bedside, comforting him and giving orders for his treatment. But she could not, or at least did not, stay the night at the castle — she was accompanied by her half-brother Moray, Huntly, Atholl, Rothes, three bishops and sundry judges, and Hermitage was hardly equipped to entertain such company. So she turned and rode back to Jedburgh, all in the same day.

Anyone who knows anything of that country, or can read a map, will realise what a feat of horsemanship this was for any woman — how the bishop got on is not reported — almost 60 miles on horseback over hill and bog and roadless wilderness, fording rivers and threading wild forested uplands. Mary was a tall, lively and energetic creature, but this must have taxed her to the utmost, especially as the weather turned wet and wild. At any rate, she fell ill with a fever at Jedburgh and lay there prostrate, as did her lover at Hermitage. And, of course, in later years of captivity in England she was known to have signed many times — 'Would that I had died at Jedworth!'

Inchdrewer Castle and
the White Dog

Standing stark and stout on a long bare ridge three miles above the pleasant town of Banff, Inchdrewer Castle surveys a wide and varied prospect of hill and coast, farmland and wood, and has done for a long time, of course. But it has a roof on it again now, and plenishings within — and it did not have either a few years ago. This is one of those castles which so greatly delight me, restored from ruin and an occupied house once more. It is a splendid bonus, from the five volumes of my *Fortified House in Scotland* series, that I have had some little hand in bringing about this happy state of affairs in well over fifty cases.

Inchdrewer was restored by a London heraldic expert, Robin de la Lanne-Mirrlees, he having some family interest therein. We corresponded on the subject, over the months; and in due course, when most of the work was done and the castle wind-and-water-tight again, although not fully furnished and completed, Mr Mirrlees held a house-warming party to celebrate, and kindly invited my wife and myself to attend. I could not manage to go up to Banff at that time; and Mr Mirrlees, who was eager for me to see the progress made after all the discussion, wrote suggesting that I make a point of visiting Inchdrewer next time I was in the North of Scotland. The Banff builder, Mr Sandy Walker, responsible for all the good work, had a key and would let me have it for an inspection.

Well, my wife and I were up in these parts a few months later, working on one of the *Queen's Scotland* volumes, and we duly made a call on Mr Walker at his yard in Banff. Instead of handing over the key, he most kindly insisted on conducting us up to the castle in person and showing us over, being quite proud of his labours — as well he might be.

We arrived at the castle doorway, the only one and strong, as is the way with fortified houses, and he inserted the key and opened the massive door. And immediately, out trotted a large white dog, a Samoyed I believe is the breed, shaggy-coated but well-groomed and clean. This substantial animal scarcely glanced at us as it ran off, out into the flanking field and away. It seemed to know where it was going, although there was no house in sight.

Our builder-friend burst out with exclamatory concern. What in the name of all that was wonderful was this?

Where had that brute come from? He had never seen it before, or the like. How had it got in? Nobody else had a key save Mr de la Lanne-Mirrlees in London. And it was a week since he had been up to the castle. The creature must have sneaked in then, somehow, unseen — although how he could not imagine. There would be goodness-knows what sort of a mess and smell inside.

Well, we went in — and there were no messes, no smells, no indication that a large dog had been shut up alone in the place for a week. There were no open windows, nor indeed openings of any sort low enough for dog or man to get in — naturally enough in a castle. Utterly at a loss, Mr Walker could scarcely demonstrate all the points and problems of his restoration work for wondering about the confounded dog.

We were greatly impressed by all that we saw, and in hearing what was intended still should be done at Inchdrewer; but the thought of that animal rather preoccupied us also, I must admit. We puzzled over it, then and later, but never came up with any valid answer.

Some months later, however, there was an echo of sorts. A copy of the magazine *Vogue* arrived by post, sent by Mr Mirrlees. This contained an illustrated article about his fine London house in Holland Park which had apparently recently been redecorated in remarkable fashion with large mural paintings of classical scenes in which the figures were given the features of sundry of Mr Mirrlees' friends. There was a lot about this; but at the end was a brief paragraph which informed readers that the owner also possessed various other houses in other countries, including a recently-restored small castle in Scotland which was reputed to be haunted by a lady in the shape of a white dog.

As to that, your guess is as good as mine.

Incidentally, in the 16th and 17th centuries Inchdrewer had been the seat of a branch of the Ogilvie family of Dunlugas, one of whom was created Viscount Banff in 1642. In 1713 a tragedy occurred here, when George,

Lord Banff, was murdered, it was thought by thieving servants, who thereupon set fire to the building to try to conceal their crime. The castle was evidently rebuilt, for it was said to be entire when the eighth viscount, and last, died in 1803. I have uncovered no account of a spectral lady, and await further elucidation.

Innischonnel Castle and
its Imprisoned Child

This castle is less well-known than it deserves to be, for it has a resounding history and is not remotely situated. Even travellers and tourists eager to inspect all that is interesting often pass it by unnoticed. This is because it sits on a tiny island towards the head of Loch Awe — that is, the south-western end, often referred to erroneously as the foot — very close to the shore and the main road, about ten miles north-east of Ford, Argyll. It is not readily seen, however, because of intervening trees and the fact that the castle itself is largely overgrown with ivy.

Although it has long been a roofless ruin, Innischonnel's walls remain fairly complete and its main features are retained — a simple structure, approximately rectangular, with lofty curtain-walls and square towers at opposite angles. No bridge links it with the mainland. It was the original seat of the great family of the Campbells of Lochow (as it used to be spelled) and of Argyll, and still belongs to MacCailean Mhor, the Duke of Argyll, who now lives at Inveraray, some miles across the hills to the east.

Although the somewhat misty Dairmid O'Duine is usually accepted as the founder of the line, the progenitor from whom the Campbell Chief takes his proud title of MacCailean Mhor, was Big Colin, who was slain at the Red Ford in Lorn in 1294; and since this castle dates from that 13th century, no doubt it was his seat. But it became more famous when, during the Wars of Independence, the Bruce's friend and brother-in-law, Sir Neil Campbell of Lochow, was the Chief — although he can have spent little time on his tiny island in all his toing-and-froing across the breadths of Scotland in his support of the hero-king. With the powerful MacDougalls based nearby, and in opposition to Bruce, this stronghold must have seen stirring events in that vital period of Scotland's story.

But perhaps Innischonnel's most extraordinary tale concerns a later time, when in 1484, the child-heir to the mighty Lordship of the Isles, Donald Dubh, or Dark, was kidnapped by Colin Campbell, first Earl of Argyll, from his home on the Isle of Islay, after the disastrous Battle of Bloody Bay, off Mull, and brought here to commence an imprisonment which lasted until the infant had grown to manhood, incredible as this may seem. Donald was 19 when at last he was rescued by a band of Glencoe MacDonalds, who secretly crossed the Campbell country, rowed across to the island and rushed the castle, to free their Chief, whose whole life had hitherto been confined

to this building. He was thereafter proclaimed King of the Isles, and he raised the standard of revolt against the government of James IV, in which Argyll was a leading light. It is interesting to note the names of those who supported his rising — the Macleans of Duart and Ardgour, the MacLeods of Lewis and Dunvegan, MacNeil of Barra, MacLaine of Lochbuie, MacIan of Ardnamurchan, the Mackinnon, the MacQuarrie, and of course all the MacDonalds and MacDonells, Clanranald, Glengarry, Knoydart, Lochaber, Sleat, Islay and the rest. Yet despite all this, the rising was put down, and King James adopted the Lordship of the Isles into the Scots crown, where it has remained, despite efforts to retrieve it — the present Lord of the Isles being none other than Prince Charles, Duke of Rothesay and Prince of Wales.

Donald Dubh was captured again, and subjected to an even longer term of imprisonment, no less than 38 years this time, in the somewhat larger castle of Edinburgh, plots to free him of no avail. However, although now a man of 60, who had spent only three years of his life in freedom, he eventually contrived to escape. And once again the Hebrides rose in his support. Henry VIII sent the exiled Earl of Lennox, Darnley's father, to aid him. But failure again; and although this time Donald was not captured but managed to flee to Ireland, there he died shortly afterwards, allegedly of a broken heart, poor man. And that marked the end of the MacDonald supremacy of the Hebrides and the West Highland mainland.

At what stage the so-successful Campbell Chiefs left Innischonnel to remove their headquarters to Inveraray is not clear — there was an Inveraray Castle considerably before the present one was built in 1744. But MacCailean Mhor still returns to Innischonnel's ancient walls for special celebrations, it is good to know.

We may wonder whether such affairs are ever haunted by the wraith of Donald Dubh?

Killochan Castle and the Lord's Work

The green and sylvan valley of the Girvan Water in Carrick is a highly attractive area of Ayrshire, rich in fine estates and ancient lairdships, very much Kennedy country. But Killochan, situated about three miles from Girvan, was not a Kennedy house, and managed to escape the acquisitive clutches of that forceful clan down the centuries — which says something positive about its owners, the Cathcarts. It is an excellent and indeed dramatic example of a Scots fortalice of the late 16th century, that most successful and productive period of all castle-building activity, a tall and handsome combination of stronghold and comfortable dwelling-house, all now mellowed by the ages.

Like so many others it is built on the L-plan, with a circular tower at one corner and angle-turrets projecting at the gables, with shot-holes piercing the walling. A device called a machicolation, for pouring down unpleasantness upon unwelcome visitors, projects high above the doorway in the angle of the L. But despite these reminders of defensive strength and wha-dare-meddle-wi'-me, so necessary in Kennedy country, it is a commodious house with fine rooms, excellent panelling, good wide stairways and ample domestic quarters; also wall-chambers, or garde-robes, for sanitation. But, just in case anyone forgot, there is the typical small and unpleasant pit or prison, for the baron to exercise his authority of the pit-and-gallows on those who countered his purposes and were caught. In this case it is known as the Thieves' Hole. There is also an ingenious hiding-place, reached from the attic storey. Over the doorway is inscribed on the lintel: 'The name of the Lord is ane strong tour and the rytheous in thair troublis rinnis into it and findith refuge. Proverbs 18 Vers 10.'

Above this pious and very practical quotation is another inscription: 'This work was Begun the 1 of Marche 1586 be Ihone Cathcart of Carleton and Helene Wallace his Spous.' Still higher is a heraldic panel bearing the arms of Cathcart and Wallace. The Cathcarts were a godly lot. Here is their story.

As their name might suggest, they were originally vassals of the High Stewards of Scotland. In 1178 Ranaldus de Kethcart witnessed a charter by Walter Dapifer Regis, that is Walter the High Steward, to the Abbey of Paisley. Cathcart itself, of course, is in Renfrewshire, where also was the Steward's main seat. In 1307 we read, in Barbour's *Bruce*, of the early victory of Loudoun Hill:

> '*A knight that then was in his rout*
> *Worthy and witht, stalwart and stout,*
> *Courteous and fair, and of good fame,*
> *Sir Alan Cathcart was his name.*'

This Sir Alan was married to a sister of Sir Duncan Wallace of Sundrum, kinsman of the Patriot. His great-great-grandson was created Lord Cathcart in 1460 and was Warden of the West March. His great-grandson, Robert, married the heiress of the Cathcarts of Carleton and Killochan, a cadet branch, and fell at Flodden with both his elder and younger brothers. It was this Robert's grandson, John, who commenced the erection of the present castle in 1586, their earlier fortaclice having stood further up the riverside.

The Cathcarts were early supporters of the Reformation, and the builder John's signature was one of those on

the famous 'Band' of 1562 which resulted from John Knox's visit to Ayrshire to rouse the nobility and gentry to defend the Protestant cause. Again, along with a number of Kennedy lairds, he subscribed another Bond five years later to oppose Mary Queen of Scots and Bothwell before the Battle of Carberry Hill. So he certainly took his faith seriously. This of course had its useful side too, when it came to sharing out the vast Church lands taken over by the victorious Reformers.

John's grandson Hew was another fighter for the faith, a strong supporter of the Covenanters against Charles II's attempts to impose Episcopacy on the land. The historian of the times, Robert Wodrow, gives a telling description of the Cathcart laird as being 'wonderfully holy and heavenly in his family, and extraordinary in solving cases of conscience.' In a history of the Galloway sheriffs, family worship in the hall of Killochan is presented thus:

'The family convened and cushions being cast down, and

then being called out of his closet he went to worship and prayed both earnestly and confidently, after which he retired to his chamber without ever taking notice who was in the hall till meat was set upon the table, and then he came out and welcomed his guests very kindly.' At least he did provide cushions for tired knees.

His son John seems to have been of the same mettle, and held one of the banned conventicles in the hall at Killochan, at which the famous Ayrshire Covenanter John Stevenson was present, and when, he declared, he first fell in love with the Word. As a result of this, and because he had not signed a declaration against Conventicles, the Scots Privy Council in 1678 ordered a garrison of 40 horse and 120 foot to occupy Killochan. This was just too much, even for a Cathcart, and he hurriedly signed before the army arrived. Sadly, after all this, he died on the night of his marriage to a daughter of Sir George Maxwell of Pollock.

He was succeeded at Killochan by his brother Hew, who at the Glorious Revolution of 1688, which saw the end of Catholic James VII and II and the arrival of the Protestant William and Mary, raised troops in support of the Protestant cause. All this sacrifice for the faith had its reward in 1703, when Hew was created a baronet. He was Member of Parliament for Ayrshire, until in 1707, the Scottish Parliament passed into history.

The sixth and last Cathcart baronet died in 1916, after which Killochan was sold.

Lennoxlove and Britannia

This famous and handsome house in East Lothian, near Haddington, is now the seat of the Duke of Hamilton, and open to the public; interesting in many ways, not least in that it suffered a change of name, for it was originally called Lethington. The lands belonged at first to the Gifford family, Norman importees of David I; but presumably passing from them to a line which took their name from the property itself — although perhaps these were of Gifford extraction also — a branch of which became the Lethingtons, or Livingtons, of Saltcoats, another castle in this area near Gullane. However that may be, the Maitlands bought Lethington in the 14th century. Possibly the oldest work in the castle dates from that early period, but the building was much enlarged and added to down the centuries, most of the great square towers dating from the 15th century, although over the doorway is a Latin inscription describing improvements made by John Maitland, first Earl of Lauderdale, in 1626.

This family of course played a very considerable, if not always reputable, role in Scotland's story — and still does, very reputably now, the present Earl of Lauderdale being notable for his initiation and leadership of the admirable and ecumenical annual pilgrimage of Christian worship. William Maitland, Younger of Lethington will be remembered as the celebrated but less than stable Secretary of State of Mary Queen of Scots who was involved in the murder of Darnley and married one of the Queen's Maries, Mary Fleming, but eventually, rebelled against the Lords of the Congregation, was captured in Edinburgh Castle but died it is thought by poison, self-administered. His brother was even more influential, becoming successively Commendator of Coldinghame, Keeper of the Privy Seal, Secretary of State and, in 1587, Chancellor of the Realm, that is, prime-minister and created Lord Thirlstane, the name of his seat in Lauderdale before he inherited his 90-year-old father's house of Lethington.

Lord Thirlestone's son John was created Earl of Lauderdale, he who much improved this castle. He was succeeded by his son, another John, of a very different character, who in fact became 'the uncrowned king of Scotland', a man of great ability but elastic conscience. He joined the Covenanters against Charles I, but later supporting Charles II, became Secretary of State like his forebears. Only now, with the monarch resident in England, he was in fact able to rule Scotland for that less than conscientious monarch, bearing the royal commission and being created Duke of Lauderdale. His regime was notable for corruption and venality, aided and abetted by his second wife, Elizabeth Murray, Countess of Dysart — of whose activities perhaps the less said the better. When the Duke died in 1682, his body was interred in a lead coffin in the underground crypt of the large St. Mary's Church, Haddington, sometimes erroneously called The Lamp of Lothian. It was there said by the local folk that Satan never allowed Lauderdale to rest in peace, for the coffin, despite its leaden weight, kept shifting around. This, in fact, was because of the periodic flooding by the River Tyne close by the crypt, invading it and creating havoc.

But perhaps the most intriguing tale of Lethington is its change of name. This was occasioned by the fact that the beautiful Frances Stewart, daughter of an impoverished Scots Lord Blantyre, and educated in France at the court of Louis XIV, transferred to the court of Charles II at London, where she quickly attracted the attentions of that womanising monarch, and gained the nickname of La Belle Stewart. She was in due course created Duchess of Lennox. However, she presently tired of Charles and eloped with his illegitimate son, or one of them, by Louise de Kerouaille, the Duke of Richmond. When she died, she left a large fortune to her cousin, another hard-up Lord Blantyre, whom she favoured, and with it he acquired Lethington on which he had set his heart — and which, according to the terms of her Will, he was to rename Lennoxlove. La Belle Stewart it was who served

as the model for the picture of Britannia, Ruler of the Waves, which came to be used, and well-known, in the coinage. A magnificent silver toilet service with the monogram and coronet of the lady was found in the attic of the castle in 1900, but is now in the Royal Scottish Museum, Edinburgh.

Lennoxlove is still, however, full of treasures, including the death-mask of Mary Queen of Scots and the silver casket which once contained the famous Casket Letters, written to Bothwell by Mary, and which themselves featured in history notoriously.

Lochleven Castle and a Queen's Tragedy

S ited on a small island in Loch Leven, the freshwater one in Kinross-shire in Central Scotland, is this medium-scale castle with a large-scale history. So much has happened here, rather surprisingly, considering its situation, size and difficulty of access. For although it is only a quarter-mile from the shore, and less than a mile from the town of Kinross, it can be reached only by a small boat; and in the old days, with horse-travel obligatory, it must have been inconvenient to reach indeed. Therefore, of course, the more secure from attack.

It was used as a royal hunting-seat in the 12th and 13th centuries; but the present building dates from the 15th century, a simple square tower of five storeys and a garret, formerly standing within a curtain-walled court-yard, with secondary outbuildings, some of which remain. Almost all the islet was thus occupied.

Alexander III and his young queen, Margaret, were forcibly carried off from here to Stirling in 1257. In 1301, during the Wars of Independence, it was besieged by the English, but relieved by The Red Comyn, whom The Bruce later slew. Archibald, Earl of Douglas died a prisoner herein in 1429. And the first archbishop Scotland had, Patrick Graham, Primate, of St. Andrews, was held captive here by his jealous eneinies, and died at Loch Leven in 1477. Even the English 7th Earl of Northumberland, who had conspired against his own monarch, Queen Elizabeth, was held prisoner here before being handed over for execution by her in 1572. By this time, the castle had passed out of royal hands into those of the Douglas family, head of which was the Earl of Morton, Regent for the infant James VI.

No doubt it was this connection which, ensured by immuring another royal captive, gave Lochieven Castle its most stirring but pathetic story. For here was incarcerated the beautiful but tragic Mary Queen of Scots, after her capture by the Lords of the Congregation at the Battle of Carberry Hill in 1567, when she was deserted by the Earl of Bothwell, her third husband, and placed in the keeping of some of her harshest enemies, including the Earl of Morton — and those Protestant lords could be harsh indeed. She was aged only 25, and had been returned to Scotland from her upbringing in France only six years before, for her short but highly dramatic reign. Her year-old son, James, was held by the lords in Stirling Castle.

Mary makes a tragic figure indeed. It was her misfortune to be the only queen-regnant, as distinct from queen-consort, to have to rule her troublesome realm, just when the Reformation had finally succeeded — and she a fervent Catholic. She tried very hard to be a good monarch, she was kind-hearted, courageous as well as beautiful, and meant well; but undoubtedly she lacked judgement, especially perhaps in her choice of men. But it must be remembered that she was only a girl of 19 when she had to take on the rule of her unruly kingdom, and with no experience in the art of government. Her's was an almost hopeless task. And with the Protestant divines, such as John Knox and Andrew Melville, to deal with, as well as the said lords, most of whom had done very well out of gaining the former great Church lands and did not want to have to yield them up again, Mary's position was all but untenable.

It had to come to rebellion and civil war in the end, and it was the lords who had the armed men in greatest numbers. So the Queen was defeated, taken and shut up in Lochleven Castle, and there treated with shameful rigour. Her person and even her life was threatened by her gaolers, by the Lord Ruthven in particular. She was pregnant again, to Bothwell, and in her physical and mental distress she miscarried of twins, and fell gravely ill. In this state she was forced to sign a deed of abdication in favour of her infant son, who thus became James VI at one year old. Poor Mary!

But help of a sort was at hand, for she did have friends, even though her husband had fled, after Carberry, to Denmark, where he eventually died. The most effective of her supporters were the Lord Seton and Sir Thomas Kerr of Fernihurst (whom Mary called her Protector) and these, with others, ever sought to contrive the Queen's release from bondage. As it happened, a son of the keeper of Lochleven, George Douglas, and a kinsman named Will Douglas, had both come under Mary's spell — for she was a highly attractive woman — and they were in a good position to assist in her escape — although the first attempt thereat was unsuccessful. But, trying again one night, during the father Sir William Douglas's birthday celebrations, the young men managed to smuggle the Queen out, dressed as a serving-woman, with the help of John Beaton, Younger of Creich, a nephew of the late Cardinal Beaton. They locked the castle doors behind them, throwing the keys down the mouth of one of the castle's cannons. In a small boat, Mary lying flat on the bottom to be inconspicuous, they rowed her to a lonely part of the loch-shore, where Lord Seton and Kerr were waiting with horses. The Queen was free again — although not for very long.

They took her to Niddry Castle, near Winchburgh in West Lothian, one of Seton's seats, and she renounced her abdication-under-duress. From there she sought to muster her supporters in strength, and made for the West, where she was strongest. But before she was fully prepared, the Lords of the Congregation, under her

half-brother the Earl of Moray, descended upon her gathering forces and defeated them at the Battle of Langside, near Glasgow, 11 days after her escape from Lochleven. This time Mary was not captured, but fled southwards into Galloway with a few of her closest friends. And at Dundrennan Abbey she slept her last night in her own kingdom, for next day, against the advice of her supporters, she decided to go and throw herself on the mercy of her sister-monarch and kinswoman, Queen Elizabeth of England. She set sail across Solway, to Cumberland. We all know the result — a score of years of captivity in English prisons and then execution on Elizabeth's orders in 1587, aged 45.

Mary Stewart must often have wished that she had died at Lochleven Castle, as she nearly did. We often hear her quoted as saying 'Would that I had died at Jedworth!' It could equally well have been Lochleven.

Luftness Castle and the Locked Door

There are few occupied Scottish houses with so long, varied and important a background-story as Luffness, standing in its woodland setting at the head of Aberlady Bay, between the villages of Aberlady and Gullane in East Lothian. For although today Luffness looks like a fairly typical late-16th century fort-alice of moderate size, looks are in this case misleading. Luffness Castle, in fact, dates from the 12th century, when it was one of the most important and major strongholds in southern Scotland, one of the 'keys of the kingdom' indeed, greater and more powerful than most. And the signs and vestiges of that strength are still there to be seen. Not only that, but there are fascinating indications of still earlier importance, preceding this Norman stone-castle influence and dating back to Celtic-Viking times. For under the floor of the vaulted basement chamber, now the entrance-vestibule, are the graves of two Viking raiders, from one of whom, Lofda, Luffness takes its name — Lofda's Point or Nose. The circumstances of these two being buried here we can only guess; but Lofda himself must have been an important man of his kind. Possibly an enormous man, for when the skeletons were dug up and then re-interred during a re-building, the bones of one indicated that he must have been seven feet tall. We know that Anlaf the Dane, a greatly-feared Viking, was operating in these parts in the mid-10th

century, so that probably Lofda was one of his lieu-
tenants. So this site must have been of significance even
a thousand years ago.

The great stronghold, however, was built by one of the
semi-royal line of the Cospatrick Earls of Dunbar, related
to Malcolm Canmore, and to whom that King gave practically all Lothian and the Merse — if he could tame it,
for it was then a very difficult land to control from the
Celtic royal houses's power-base north of Forth. The
great moat and angle-tower bases of this huge castle still
remain, although the enclosing curtain-walls have gone.

Why these have disappeared is a story in itself. In
1547, during the Rough Wooing period of the child-
queen Mary, Henry VIII of England sent up an army
under the Earl of Hertford, in one of his many attempts
to grasp the infant monarch, and Scotland with her.
Hertford on this occasion got repulsed from Edinburgh,
retired on Haddington and there was besieged. Henry
had to send up a fleet to try to relieve his force. This
entered Aberlady Bay, then much deeper and more
extensive than now, Aberlady being the port of
Haddington. Mary of Guise sent General de Thermes,

one of her French mercenaries, to Luffness Castle, to repel the invaders, and he set up an earthen bank to the north of the moat, facing into the bay, on which to site his cannon. That bank is still there. This defence was successful and the fleet was driven off, and went to Blackness to wreak its resentment there. Henry was furious, and although he died that same year, he set in train a much greater army, which in 1549 came north and won the fatal Battle of Pinkie, near Musselburgh. The terms imposed on the defeated Scots included one de manded by Henry before his death, that Luffness Castle should be 'spoiled', in other words, demolished, in vengance. This was attempted by the victorious English, and although they managed to pull down the curtain-walls and the top storeys of the keep, the ten-foot-thick walls of the latter were too much for them, and these still remain and form the two lower storeys of the present castle, the upper works of which were rebuilt in 1584, and give the castle its present outline. The vaulted basements of the angle-towers for the great enclosure remain today as green mounds, their vaults intact beneath the grass, witnesses to the vast extent of this once-huge stronghold.

There are innumerable stories about Luffness, but the one which I shall recount here relates to one of these vaulted basements, but in the keep itself, not in an angle-tower. This one was the porter's lodge, as these places were called, a stone-vaulted small chamber guarding the original entrance to the keep, with no windows but with splayed gun-loops opening at about four feet from floor level, for defence. This chamber was in modern times not much used by the Hope family, who have owned Luffness since 1713, but sometimes did duty as a spare cloakroom — as it was windowless, it was not very convenient for most purposes, and there were plenty of other rooms. But it had a massive ancient door and great lock and key, although the door normally stood open.

Well, one day not so very many years ago, the son of the house, coming down, discovered the door locked and the key missing. The whole family and household were astonished, for nobody admitted to having locked the door nor could think of any reason for anyone doing so. The door was far too heavy to break down without a major upheaval, so it was left. Then one day the son thought of shining a torch in through one of the gun-loops. These are splayed outside and in, for giving a greater range of fire, but the central aperture is only about three inches across. At any rate, when the beam shone into the dark vault through there, it was to reveal, at approximately the same level as the gun-loop, the great iron key projecting from the ancient lock, on the inside.

Nothing else is to be seen, save an old table on which coats occasionally were put. Owing to the position of the gun-loops it is impossible to depress or raise the light beam to floor or vaulted ceiling. That key is still there, inside. The Hopes have never sought to break down the massive door, feeling that their ancient house is entitled to its own secrets — but so far as is known nobody is missing!

Mearns Castle and the Kirk

Many castles suffer sadly at the hands of time and uncaring generations, their vicissitudes sometimes the source of stories. But I know of no other to have become, as Mearns has, a church in modern times, a most happy fate. And apt, for so long ago as the 12th century the lands of Mearns were given to Holy Church and the Abbey of Paisley, although they were soon back in secular hands.

Mearns is situated, not in The Mearns of Kincardineshire, but in Renfrewshire, in the ever-growing community of Newton Mearns, seven miles south-west of Glasgow and now almost a suburb, taking its name therefrom. The castle stands on a strong defensive site overlooking quite a steep valley; and although now only a square keep of four storeys and a garret, once had its curtain-walls, courtyard, defensive gatehouse, drawbridge and moat, all of the 15th century. In this case such is no mere architectural conjecture, for we have the details. James II, in 1449, gave the Lord Maxwell, whose family had acquired the property by marriage with the Pollock heiress around 1300, a licence to erect and fortify a castle, with declared stipulations as to what and how. In fact, there must have been a previous stronghold on the site for, in a most unusual feature, the lowermost courses of the keep are built in a rough rubble masonry, above which starts the fine ashlar, or squared stone blocks of the 15th century, both reaching a thickness of ten feet. The castle is again rather unusual in having the first floor, as well as the basement, vaulted. This vaulting is notably high, providing space for an intermediate timber floor, known as an entresol — though this has long gone. The high vaulting, of course, is particularly suitable for church purposes.

The Maxwells were a vehement and enduring line. Nowadays people tend to associate them mainly with Dumfriesshire and the West March of the Borders. But they came originally from the Kelso area of Roxburgh, in the east, where the ancient parish of Maxwell was, along with the similar names of Maxton, Makerstoun and Maxpoffle, all being associated with one Maccus, who flourished about 1140. There was a Maccus, lord of part of the Hebrides in 973, so the name is probably Celtic. At any rate, they cut a wide swathe in Scotland and their story could fill this book. The third lord, John, fell with James IV at Flodden. His son, the Lord Robert, was Scots ambassador to France, fought at the dire battle of Solway Moss, was captured and taken to imprisonment in the Tower of London and there languished for long before he was ransomed. The sixth lord managed to obtain the earldom of Morton at the execution and forfeiture of the notorious Regent Morton in 1581, but was deprived of it and killed in the great battle with the Johnstones in 1593, the largest clan-battle in Scots history and not Highland at all. In consequence, his son, the seventh lord, in turn slew Sir James Johnstone of that Ilk in 1608, and was executed for the deed. And so on. In 1589 James VI, resenting the Maxwell power, ordered Lord Herries, a subsidiary title of the family, to yield up to him Mearns Castle and sundry other strengths. Seventy years later the Earl of Nithsdale — to which status the Lords Maxwell had now risen — must have found his new rank expensive, for he sold Mearns to another of the family, Sir George Maxwell of Nether Pollock. So, strangely, it came back to the lairdship from which it had started — just as it was fated to come back still further, to the church.

Thus, in modern times, the castle was no longer lived

in but still fairly intact as far as parapet-level of the keep. Indeed, we read in a publication of 1842 that it was still used occasionally 'for balls given by the Mearns troop of the lately-disembodied yeomanry cavalry of Renfrewshire, which numbered among its officers several members of the distinguished family to which the castle belonged.' It was in this condition when I wrote about and sketched it for my third volume of *The Fortified House in Scotland*, in 1964. Then, in 1973, came the decision to save it and make it the centre-piece of a parish-church complex of chapel, hall and manse, to my delight. The area was being steadily developed, of course, with everspreading new housing, so near to Glasgow. The minister concerned corresponded with me and explained their plans, how the main first floor vaulted hall was to be the chapel, with the organ installed suitably in the minstrel's gallery, which had been contrived in the access from the turnpike stairway to the now-gone entresol floor. The ground-floor vault was to be turned into a kitchen area, with toilets and cloakrooms; and the upper floors for community-room purposes, all with terrazzo flooring, lighting and heating.

Here then is a story with a happy ending — or rather, not an ending so much as a new beginning. All credit to the minister, kirk session and congregation of the Church of Maxwell Mearns Castle for the imagination, initiative and courage involved. May I add my own text, for others? 'Go thou and do likewise!'

Megginch Castle and
the Secret Passage

The Carse of Gowrie is now a most fertile littoral of the Tay's north bank, snug with fine farmlands and tree-girt estates, looking a scene of ancient peace. But it was not always so, as the very name Megginch reveals — for this is but a corruption of the Gaelic Maol-g-inch, meaning the bald or bare island. And since Megginch is a mile inland from the Tay, it indicates that this was an island, not in the estuary but in marshland. Before drainage became general, the Carse, like much level land below hills — in this case the Sidlaws — was largely bog, something we are apt to forget these days, roadless and wild, with the roads having to keep up on the higher ground. So, although Megginch Castle does not present the appearance of a highly defensive site today, among its fine, level parks and woodlands, it was once secure indeed, islanded among spreading marshes and pools, or pows as they were called, as effective as any moat.

The castle is a picturesque and venerable pile, with angle-turrets and circular stair-tower, the roof somewhat lowered from the original. Like so many others, it was largely built in the second half of the 16th century, with James VI's edict that 'tours of fence' must be erected on all properties worth more than £100 Scots per annum — this in a laudable but somewhat mistaken effort to provide security for the lieges by establishing a host of small castles all over the country, to which they could flee for refuge in lawless times; whereas, of course, what happened was that in a great many cases the lairds turned these new fortalices into holds from which they could oppress the said lieges, with little danger of being winkled out. I am not saying, mind you, that this was the case with Megginch Castle.

It was a Hay property from the second half of the 15th century. The Hays were a very powerful family in the Carse of Gowrie, William the Lyon having given great lands here to William de Haya. Two generations later, Sir Gilbert Hay of Erroll was the great supporter and friend of Robert the Bruce who made him High Constable of Scotland. In 1452 his great-great-great-grandson William was created Earl of Erroll — the little town of Errol (usually spelled with only one L) which sits doucely in the Carse, hidden from the main road less than two miles

south of Megginch. The first Hay of Megginch was a kinsman, Peter by name, who died before 1496. How much of his 15th century castle is incorporated in the present building is hard to say, for there was a great rebuilding a century later; indeed a lintel over one of the windows is inscribed PETRUS HAY AEDIFICIUM EXTRUXIT AN 1575. The overall aspect of the house is certainly of this period.

The Hays did not for very long enjoy their rebuilding, however. For around 1636 William, tenth Earl of Erroll, by his extravagance and support of Charles I, had to sell his Carse lands; and this declension seems to have affected his kinsman, Sir George, at Megginch also, for in 1640 the castle and lands were sold to the Drummonds — who, happily, are still very much there. They had come from Strathearn, the Drummond homeland, not so very far away on the other side of Perth; where John Drummond, the new laird of Megginch, was eighth feudal baron of Lennoch and Hereditary Seneschal of Strathearn. The Carse of Lennoch lies between Crieff and Comrie, at the foot of its glen which is usually called Glen Lednock.

The Drummonds were, and still are, a lively lot, and Megginch has had its excitements. They were notable enemies of the MacGregors, which in itself was apt to ensure developments. This feud stemmed from the murder, in 1589, of John Drummond of Drummond Ernoch, in the Forest of Glenartney, by the MacGregors. This Drummond was the King's Forester of Glenartney. It was a particularly barbarous deed, for the MacGregors, after slaying him, cut off his head and carried it down to the house of Ardvorlich, where the Stewart laird's wife was Drummond's sister. The laird being out, the MacGregor's demanded bread and cheese, and while the lady of the house was getting this, they took the bloody head out of a plaid, set it on the table, and when the bread and cheese came, stuffed it into the dead man's mouth. Not unnaturally the lady shrieked and fled the house, into the woods, whereupon the MacGregors took the head to their own glen of Balquhidder, and there, before the Laird of MacGregor and his assembled clan, all swore on the head itself to defend the authors of the deed — sufficient excuse for a Highland feud, you may allow? This was part of the reason for James VI's outlawing of the MacGregors and the proscribing of the name.

The Drummonds had long memories, for the third Drummond of Megginch was still hot against the MacGregors a century and a half later, and very active in hunting them down after the failure of the Rising of 1715. This, in a way, was odd, for of course the Drummonds in general had been among the greatest supporters of the Old Pretender. Lord Drummond himself having been lodged in the Tower of London in 1708 for his Jacobite sympathies — the same who later was created Jacobite Duke of Perth; and the Drummonds had their own regiment in the Jacobite army. Indeed Drummond of Logiealmond is reported to have slain no fewer than 16 government dragoons with his own sword, before being captured at the Battle of Sheriffmuir. But this Megginch was firmly on the other side, and very unpopular with the rest of his clan. He was the first Member for Perthshire in the new London parliament after the Union of 1707. We read that his son Adam Drummond lived elsewhere, and when a nephew John eventually succeeded to Megginch he complained that it was in a bad state with 'the doos in all the rooms'.

Later lairds were prominent in various walks of life, Sir Adam being a noted admiral at the end of the 18th century and his brother, General Sir Gordon, a foremost commander during the American War of Independence. The present laird's father some years ago succeeded to the ancient title of Lord Strange.

Now a little personal anecdote. The present good Drummonds at one time told me that their castle had its underground passage. I had heard this story about so many, and despite visiting and inspecting many hundreds of fortalices and towers, had yet actually to see such a thing, that I was somewhat sceptical. It is one of the most cherished fantasies about such places, among owners and others. Time and again I have asked to be shown one. And the excuse is usually that it is, of course, now blocked up, or fallen in, or otherwise unshowable. Sometimes I have been shown semi-subterranean vaulted chambers, which it is alleged are the beginning of tunnels — but nevertheless have solid masonry ends and have been either wine-cellars, chill meat-storages or even ovens. Sometimes the tales are that these reputed tunnels go for almost miles, and manage to conquer the most improbable terrain in the process, valleys, bogs and so on.

Well, my kind hosts at Megginch were unable to show me just where their's began, or ended, and I fear that I was unconvinced. Until, some time later, they unfortunately had a fire at the castle. And one of the fire-engines, manoeuvring into position outside, part-fell into the underground tunnel.

In other words, he who laughs last laughs longest!

Melgund Castle and
the Marriage-Stone

Melgund Castle, a rose-red ruin now but still fair, set in a quietly lovely corner of Angus, near Aberlemno, seems to dream of great days, exciting days, however peaceful its present state. And it had great days, more than most — but scarcely peaceful. For it was built around 1540 by Scotland's then most powerful son, David Beaton, Cardinal-Archbishop of St. Andrews, Abbot of Arbroath and Chancellor of the

Realm for James V. And he, of course, was hardly a man of peace, despite his clerical importance. He it was, in fact, who held up the Reformation in Scotland for nearly 20 years, all but single-handed, against the machinations of England's Henry VIII. And while he was doing so, built Melgund Castle, this now serene monument to love and affection and good taste — and power.

It makes an intriguing story. Davie Beaton has been called the second most execrated name in Scots history — the first being the False Menteith who betrayed the hero Wallace. But it is as well to remember who first called him that. It was, to be sure, the Reformers, in especial John Knox, whose *History of the Reformation* is nowadays accepted as more or less gospel for that war-torn period. When he wrote it, his arch-enemy Davie was safely assassinated and the Reformers could go ahead. But just suppose that it had been the other way round, and Knox had been killed and Beaton had won the long struggle which was almost as much political as religious. Then history would have been written entirely differently. David would have been the saviour of Scotland from Henry Tudor, and Knox, Henry's pensioner, the villain. He was, after all, at the time of Beaton's slaying, chaplain to Henry's son Edward VI. No need for us to take sides in all this. But it is as well to remember that it is the winners who usually write received history, the losers tending to be dead.

Now Melgund has a lesson to teach in this respect. One of Knox's main condemnations of David Beaton is the wickedness of his private life and the numbers of his concubines and mistresses. Now I do not suggest that Davie was any sort of saint, and probably had very little of true religion in him — although undoubtedly he was a patriot. But I believe that he has been traduced, in this matter at least. Admittedly, the more you explore Angus and the Mearns, the more fine castles you will find reputedly built by the cardinal for this or that illegitimate son or daughter — which looks bad. Clearly he, a mere Fife

laird's seventh son, had amassed a vast fortune and likewise a large progeny — although men who rise to rule
nations, as he did for so long, are apt to accumulate fortunes, if not necessarily bastards. But probing into the
histories of all these family castles, one fact begins to
stand out; all these unlawful sons and daughters turn out
to be children of the one concubine — Margaret Ogilvy.
No other mistress's name crops up.

Now this puts rather a different complexion on the
story. One mistress, mother of a large family — even
though Knox described her brilliantly as Beaton's 'chief
lewd'.

We know that traditionally the cardinal built Melgund
Castle not for any of his brood, mainly by this time
grown up, but for Margaret Ogilvy herself. She was the
daughter of the first Lord Ogilvy of Airlie, ancestor of the
present Earls of Airlie and so of our Princess Alexandra's
husband. And clearly Davie Beaton loved her, and right
to the end, for this is the latest of his many buildings,
erected not so long before his death in 1546. It was, by its
size and magnificence, most evidently meant to be the
place to which he and Margaret were to retire and make
their home.

And so to the kernel of this account. A marriage-stone
was formerly built into the walling of the castle, above
one of the windows, as in so many other such edifices;
and it was carved thus, D B and M O.

These marriage-stones are of course commonplace.
There are hundreds, thousands of them still extant on
ancient Scots houses up and down the land, bearing the
initials of husband wife builders. But always, as the
name implied, they represent a marriage. Never have I
seen or heard of one which did not. D B and M O —
David Beaton and Margaret Ogilvy. Sadly I did not manage to see this stone for myself, for the castle has become
much more ruinous than a century ago when the
respected Andrew Jervise saw it and described it in his
monumental *Memorials of Angus and Mearns*, published

Menstrie Castle and the Baronets

Menstrie is a small hillfoots town, really only an industrial village, lying under the green Ochils, on the verges of Clackmannanshire and Stirlingshire, four miles from Alloa. Its castle stands in the midst of a new housing area, for which it makes a most pleasing and characterful centre. Yet this modern housing was almost the end of the castle, for the local authority was intent on pulling it down not so many years ago, it having fallen on evil days and become a mere tenement of sub-standard apartments. However a fight was put up to save it, help coming from as far away as Nova Scotia and Canada, and we eventually won the day. And now, as elsewhere that this has been achieved, the local authority is proud to have it there, a show-piece.

It is a typical L-shaped fortalice of the later 16th century, formerly surrounded by a curtain-walled courtyard. It is unusual in that the entrance to the yard was not by the normal arched gateway and gatehouse but by a pend or passage driven through the centre of the wing itself, with a handsome decorated doorway, the vaulted passage lined with stone benches. There was formerly a circular stair-tower within the angle but this has been removed, although an angle-turret with shot-holes and a small stair-turret remain. Inevitably there was much internal alteration when the castle was turned into a tenement.

Menstrie has a highly interesting history, it being built by a Highland family from Kintyre, the chieftains of Clan Allister, whom the first Earl of Argyll brought with him eastwards when he became Chancellor of Scotland at the end of the 15th century. He had to live much nearer Stirling and the court than Argyll, and so erected the famous Castle Campbell at Dollar; and the MacAllisters settled here at Menstrie about 1481, in due course anglicising their name to Alexander. No doubt there is a 15th-century nucleus in the castle, but basically it dates from the next century.

The Alexanders, in a few generations, became prosperous and powerful in the puissant shadow of the Campbells; and in 1572 was born in this house William, who was destined for great things. He was a poetic and romantic youth and at the age of 15 fell deeply in love with a local beauty — who, however, was scarcely of the rank his parents considered suitable for their son. So they sent him off as tutor to the young eighth Earl of Argyll on his foreign travels — during which young William wrote no fewer than 100 sonnets to the lady. Nevertheless, matrimony was her goal, and she in the interim was wed to a less lofty but more suitable suitor.

The young Alexander seems to have got over his disappointment, for it was not long after his return to Scotland before he was wed to a more eligible lady, the heiress of Sir William Erskine, of the Mar family. What she thought of her husband's publication, in 1604, of his first book entitled, *Aurora, Containing the First Fancies of the Author's Youth*, by W. Alexander of Menstrie, the hundred afore mentioned sonnets, is not recorded.

William went from strength to strength, poetically. Because of this, and also because he was a keen falconer, he came to the notice of James VI, who was interested in both; and when that odd monarch took over Queen Elizabeth's throne, William in due course came to London. He continued to write, but unlike so many of the poets of the day, he did not devote himself to adulation of the curious monarch but wrote on the vanity of grandeur, the abuse of power, the burden of riches and other highly moral themes. He sounds somewhat

priggish, but his activities otherw
first tragedy was founded on the
Mede, published by William Alexar
the Prince's Privy Chamber. The p
James's first-born, who died tragically
King James seems to have approved of 'r.
poet', for when this appointment ende
Henry's death, he named him Gentleman
new Prince of Wales. William's adaptabilit
by his prompt dedication, to Charles, of a lc
had in fact written in honour of his royal bro

James knighted him in 1614 and made him
Requests. Out of this arose, in 1621, a most odd
ment. The King gave him, by royal deed, a gran.
entire province of Nova Scotia — despite the fact thav
was already a French colony called Acadia, discovere.
by Cabot in 1497. Just what the young poet was expected
to do about this is not clear. But, nothing daunted, he
concocted a scheme of much ingenuity. In 1625 he published a pamphlet entitled *An Encouragement to Colonies*,
to invite adventurous settlers. But that same year James
died and it fell to the new King, Charles I, to carry out
William's great project. This involved the creation of very
welcome wealth for the Crown by the establishment of
an order of Knights-Baronet, whereby individuals who
paid the King £150 sterling for 6000 acres of Nova Scotia
should have hereditary baronetcies conferred upon
them. Thus two birds were killed with one stone, the
Crown gained necessary funds and Nova Scotia attracted
the right sort of colonists, people of substance and
wealth. A new form of lesser nobility was established,
too.

Charles was duly grateful and in 1626 he appointed Sir
William Secretary of State for Scotland and four years
later created him Viscount of Stirling; then in 1633, at his
belated coronation at Holyrood, raised him to be Earl of
Stirling.

The Earl held the office of Secretary of State for 15

was known as a moderate statesman in a vio-
d. He obviously had talents for more than poetry,
ong his many activities he got a licence from
s to coin base money, which gained him much
but considerable obloquy also, with rhymes being
e about him for a change, and rude ones too.
ewise he obtained the sole right to print and publish
e late King James's version of the Psalms for 31 years,
a rather extraordinary concession, but apparently

profitable. The Earl himself had a go at a version of the
Psalms, earlier on.

Altogether a man of parts, you will agree.

Most suitably, when Menstrie was saved a few years
ago, part of the building was set aside as a museum and
centre for the Order of Nova Scotia Baronets, of which
many holders survive to this day. The coats-of-arms of
these families, now after three and a half centuries, so
highly esteemed, decorate the walls of the Baronets'
Room.

Menstrie Castle has other claims to fame, among them

that here, in 1734, was born Sir Ralph Abercromby, the distinguished Napoleonic Wars general, victor of Aboukir Bay.

Merchiston Castle and
Enlightenment

This fine and substantial 15th-century tower-house certainly has an enduring quality about it, for although standing in a southern suburb of Edinburgh with modern building ever encroaching on every side and swallowing up its estate, it has survived sundry changes of fortune and seems now assured as to its future — although not so long ago it was threatened with demolition by municipal vandals. It has, moreover, a distinctly educational air to it, being now incorporated as the centrepiece of Napier University; and formerly, of course, served a similar role with regard to Merchiston Castle School, now at Colinton but still so-called. Perhaps this is not surprising in view of the nature and educational qualities of the most famous of its former lairds.

It is a fairly typical L-planned keep rising four storeys to a parapet and wall-walk, with a garret storey above, its walls very thick, its basement vaulted. The doorway was, and still is, not at ground level but at the first floor, formerly reached by a sort of gangway-like bridge which lifted up, and the recess for which still flanks the doorway. This was for reasons of defence, naturally. There is now a modern metal forestair. An especially interesting feature is the colourful and dramatic tempera-painted ceiling, of 1581, above the present board-room, formerly the Hall. This work of art, exceptionally frank in its anatomical detail, with witchcraft allusions, was transferred here in recent years from Prestongrange, where it was in danger of decay. There is also a fine ornamental plaster ceiling of Charles II's period.

Stories of Merchiston abound, for the Napiers were a lively family who have left a notable impression on the history of Scotland. Three of them in succession were Provosts of Edinburgh during the reigns of James II and III. Being sited right on the southern approaches to the capital, their castle was inevitably frequently involved with attacking forces, the Douglas wars being particularly difficult for Merchiston. Also it was near enough to be bombarded by the cannon of Edinburgh Castle; and in 1572 the famous Kirkcaldy of Grange, then Governor of the Castle, did just that. This was, of course, during the captivity of Mary Queen of Scots in England. It also happened to be the year of the famous John Napier's betrothal to Elizabeth Stirling of Keir. We read, of this occasion:

> 'The cumpany of Edinburgh past furth and seigit Merchingstoun; quha wan all the pairtis thairof except the dungeoun, in the quhilk wes certaine suddartis in Leith; the haill houssis wes spoulzeit and brunt, to haue smokit the men of the dungeoun out; but the cuntrie seeand the fyre, raise with the power of Leith and put the men of Edinburgh thairfra without slauchter, bot syndrie hurt.'

The old Edinburgh-Leith feud, evidently, is of ancient standing.

Later, Merchiston was used as a prison by Drury, the English commander sent up by Elizabeth Tudor to assist her pensioner, the Regent, the Earl of Morton.

John Napier's own story is as colourful and eventful as that of his castle. He was born there in 1550, and is most famous today, of course, for his invention of logarithms, for he was a brilliant mathematician. But he had many other claims to fame. An astrologer, he was regarded by his contemporaries as having supernatural powers, as witness the fact that he had a familiar spirit in the shape of a jet-black cock. That he had a sense of humour is demonstrated by his use of this famous bird. Suspecting that some missing property of his had been taken by one of his own servants, he ordered them all, one by one into one of the aforementioned dungeons, where each was required to stroke its back, having been warned that the cock would crow at the touch of the guilty hand. The cock, in fact, maintained its silence, but the hand of the thief was found to be the only one free of soot which the laird had spread on the bird, the guilty man having feared actually to touch it. On another occasion, Napier's humour took the form of swearing that he would capture alive the Laird of Roslin's pigeons which were making a nuisance of themselves in his garden. He proceeded to spread grain on the ground there, soaked in alcohol so that the birds, when they duly arrived the next day, got so drunk that he could pick them up by hand.

But his fame rests on more firm foundations than these. The philosopher David Hume described him as the person to whom the title of a great man was more

justly due than to any other whom this country had ever produced. He developed, among other inventions, the forerunner of the modern tank, a hydraulic screw for pumping water out of flooded mines and so on, and many other engineering and scientific devices, far ahead of his time. He was a theologian and metaphysician also, in 1593 interpreting the Revelation of St John the Divine.

He seems to have had his weaknesses, however, like the rest of us. For he became obsessed with the notion that there was much hidden gold to be discovered at Fast Castle, on the Berwickshire coast, a seat of the notorious Robert Logan of Restalrig, and in fact entered into a specific contract with Logan for the recovery of this alleged treasure. Part of the contract went thus:

> *'Forasmekle as ther is dywerss ald reports, motiffs and appirancis, that thar suld be within the said Robertis dwellinge place of Fastcastell a soum of monie and pois, heid and hurdit up secretlie, quhilk as yet is onfound by ony man. The said Jhone sall do his utter and exact diligens to serche and sik out, and be al craft and ingyne that he dow, to tempt, try and find out the sam ... etc.'*

John never seems to have found the Fast Castle treasure — but it is perhaps noteworthy that Logan was involved in the mysterious and murky Gowrie Conspiracy in which King James also sought very odd treasure, and it was all not so very long after the unsavoury business of the Spanish Blanks whereby a vast sum in gold allegedly came from Spain to aid Catholic forces in Scotland seeking to overturn the Reformation, in which both the King's and Logan's names were bandied about. Napier may have not been quite so daft as his spelling!

At any rate, the family went from strength to strength, treasure or none. John's son went with James to London in 1603, and thereafter held many offices of state, including that of Lord Justice Clerk, and was created first Lord Napier in due course — which peerage still survives.

Monymusk and the Reliquary

Monymusk is an ancient name, but oddly, not quite so ancient as the item which has made the name so famous in Scotland's story, the Moneymusk Reliquary. This, its true style being the Brecbennach of St. Columba, now to be seen in the Museum of Antiquities, Edinburgh, is a delightful little house-shaped casket of typical Celtic workmanship used by the Irish prince-saint who came to this country in 563 to begin his enormous task of re-introducing Christianity to the kingdoms of Alba, Dalriada and Strathclyde, which now make up Scotland, and where the faith had lapsed sadly after the mission of St. Ninian a century and a half before. The Brecbennach, used later to contain a bone of the saint, was considered to be so valuable and effective a talisman as to be carried by its custodian into battle at the head of Scots armies, and was so carried before Bruce at Bannockburn, in 1314. The year after that great victory, Bernard de Linton, Bruce's trusted chaplain and friend, Abbot of Arbroath, and almost certainly the author of the famous Declaration of Arbroath, handed over the Brecbennach to Malcolm of Monymusk, the Prior there, for safe keeping. It remained at Monymusk for 618 years.

The castle has other claims to fame, of course. Although in the main a tall and massive late 16th century towerhouse, there is earlier work incorporated, including probably some of the monastic building. For there was a priory established here until the Reformation, and an

ancient one, dating from the Celtic Church period, one of the earlier establishments of the Keledei, The Friends of God, or Culdees as the name became corrupted to, Columba's successors — so there was good reason for entrusting the Brecbennach to them. Malcolm Canmore, the slayer and successor of MacBeth, paused here in 1078, on an expedition against the rebels of Moray, MacBeth's people, and vowed that if given the victory he would donate his barony nearby to the Church, even allegedly marking out with his spear the ground for the base of the tower, a picturesque touch. More believable, we know that Gilchrist, Earl of Mar, in 1170 built a priory here for the Culdees, who still seem to have clung on in isolated places despite Canmore's wife's determination to replace the ancient Celtic Church by the Roman Catholic one, for which she was in due course turned into St Margaret. The Priory was Romanised in due course, and was taken over by the Augustinians; but relics of the Celtic/Pictish period are still to be seen in the nearby parish church of Monymusk; indeed there is a handsome Pictish sculptured-stone still built into the walling of one of the castle's downstairs apartments. It is perhaps no recommendation for the change-over to the Romish discipline, with declining standards of behaviour, that the second-last Prior, John Elphinstone, was convicted of murder! A beautiful statue of the Virgin Mary, known as the Monymusk Madonna, of possibly Flemish early 16th century workmanship, is another precious relic.

The Priory fell to the great Aberdeenshire family of Forbes at the Reformation but they held it only for about a century, for in 1712 Sir William Forbes sold Monymusk and its castle to Sir Francis Grant, known as Lord Cullen of Session, for £116,000 Scots, which seems a great sum indeed for those days. But it must be remembered that the Pound Scots was worth only one-sixth of the Pound Sterling. Lord Cullen's son, Sir Alexander Grant was a great agricultural reformer, not a religious one, who introduced turnips as a field crop for winter feed for stock, as well as other innovations. He is reputed to have planted more trees than anyone else in the British Isles, over 50 million in 50 years — and this permitted his son and grandson to sell timber to a value of over £22,000 sterling — that is, more than Lord Cullen paid for the entire property. Sir Alexander Grant was indeed a busy man. It is recorded that he wrote in his journal regarding his second wife, Anne Potts, 'My wife is a dreadful Slug-abed, 'tis oft six of a morning ere she rises.'

Muchalls Castle and the Laird's Lug

Muchalls is rather a special place, partly because of its architectural style and excellence, partly because it has remained so comparatively unaltered down the centuries, and partly because of its magnificent heraldic plaster ceilings which are scarcely to be equalled in Scotland.

It is situated on an isolated position on high ground above the Kincardine coast some four miles north of Stonehaven. As it stands it is a fine example of an early 17th century fortalice on the E-plan; that is, a main block with wings projecting at either end in the same direction, enclosing a courtyard which still retains its curtain-walling and defensive arched gateway. The crowstepped gables, the series of tall, coped chimney-stacks and the round angle-turrets add up to a highly attractive composition.

The Great Hall, on the first floor of the main block, as well as its splendid painted plaster ceiling displaying in brilliant colours the coats-of-arms of the Burnetts and other families, has an enormous fireplace, its great lintel formed out of a single piece of stone, and a handsome overmantel featuring the royal arms of James VI, flanked by caryatids. Not only so, but hidden above one of the ingle-neuks within is the aperture for a narrow shaft or duct in the thickness of the walling which communicates with a mural-chamber off the laird's bedroom directly above, where there is another aperture, whereby anyone sitting there can hear all that is said in the hall below — a notable convenience known as the laird's lug. Sometimes such ear-holes were enhanced by having a squint, or peep-hole in the Hall ceiling, but not here.

The original Muchalls Castle, of which some traces and a semi-subterranean vault remain, was a Fraser stronghold, that family having gained great possessions in this part of the country by Robert the Bruce's favour towards his supporter and brother-in-law, Sir Alexander Fraser, Great Chamberlain, who married Mary Bruce — her second husband. It is to be feared that the Frasers had deteriorated somewhat by the end of their tenure of Muchalls, for we read that in 1614 the Privy Council had to take note of the fact that Andrew Fraser, the heir of Muchalls, accompanied by George Grant, 'a noisome fighter' and others, all armed and wearing 'pistolets, dernit themselves at the Brig o' Dee,' where they attacked Alexander Bannerman of Elsick, another Kincardine laird, his son and brother, wounding the latter. Fraser was fined and his father, the Laird of Muchalls, had to find caution of 5,000 merks for future

good behaviour. The Council was moved to declare '... such ane feckles and unworthy cause as hes not been hard of in ony country subject to law and justice, to wit because the said Alex Bannerman simply and ignorantly took the place before Fraser at the ingoing of a door.'

Well, the Frasers had not much longer at Muchalls, for over the courtyard entrance is carved the following inscription. 'This work begun on the east and north be Ar. Burnet of Leyis 1619. Ended be Sir Thomas Burnet of Leyis his sonne 1627.'

So the castle as we see it today is a Burnet creation. The Burnets or de Burnards, were one of the Norman families which David I introduced into Scotland in the 12th century, becoming lairds of Fairnington in Roxburghshire. Alexander Burnard supported Bruce, as did the Frasers, and was rewarded, like them, with lands up here which had been possessed by the Comyns, Bruce's enemies. Alexander, in fact, was made keeper of the great royal forest of Drum, and the hunting-horn, which is such a feature of the Burnet arms, reminds us of this. However, Bruce later gave Drum and its keepership to his faithful armourbearer, Sir William Irvine, but compensated the Burnards with other lands nearby, at Leys. A long line of lairds followed, their name becoming first Burnet then Burnett. Their principal seat was at Crathes Castle, now the well-known National Trust for Scotland show-place, where their famous hunting-horn still hangs. Presumably they acquired and built the quite large castle of Muchalls for cadets of the Crathes line. It is noteworthy that both the fourth baronet and his brother married Burnett sisters of Muchalls.

Sir Thomas, who completed the building, was active on the Covenanting side with the great Montrose, before the latter changed over to King Charles's cause. In consequence, Muchalls was attacked by George Gordon, Viscount of Aboyne, on the other side, and 'was rifled by them the next day on ther returne; and the night that they lay ther the cornes abused and anything else as ther humors served them, whereupon they could lay ther handes, for manye of the countrye people were fledde and ther best goodes transported into the strong holde of Dunnotar not far distant.' A battle was fought next day between Muchalls and Stonehaven, where Montrose was victorious, and thereafter this countryside was restored to temporary peace. Later in the war, with Montrose now on the other side, he came victoriously this way and burned the town of Stonehaven. But Muchalls seems to have escaped — presumably because, as we read, 'Sir Thomas Burnet was that rare combination, a friend of Huntly's and a staunch Covenanter; he hospitably entertained the royal Lieutenant (Montrose) and his staff, and offered him a sum of money, which was refused.' Difficult times!

A century later, in 1746, the Duke of Cumberland, in the aftermath of Culloden, burned part of Muchalls, but happily no trace of this damage remains.

The castle no longer belongs to the Burnetts, but is still occupied, and a delightful family home.

Neidpath Castle and the March

The Borderland used to be full of peel-towers, every laird great and small possessing one — and necessarily, since a strong fortified house was a prime priority in those lawless days, and in lands ever open to English raiding in especial. Peebles-shire alone is reputed to have had over 80, of which only some five survive more or less intact, a score or so of ruins remain and the rest are mere sites, known or unknown. The same applied elsewhere on the Border. The reason for this wholesale disappearance, of course, is much the same as for their existence in the first place — the so-near presence of the hostile English. The innumerable invading forces down the centuries made a point of destroying all such behind them, partly in hate, partly as a precaution against them serving as rallying points at their backs when advancing, when they might have to hurry home unimpeded. Neidpath, towering above the Tweed a mere mile west of Peebles itself, must always have been one of the strongest of these peel-towers, and happily has survived. Although not occupied now it is kept in good condition by its owner, the Earl of Wemyss and March, and is a favourite with visitors. Latterly it was the seat of the ancient March earldom, March in this instance being the same word as Merse, merely meaning Border.

It was an early stronghold of the Fraser family, however. We tend nowadays to think of the Frasers as a Highland clan; but, like the Gordons, Chisholms and others, they started upon the Border, as Norman importees of David I, in the 12th century, and worked their way northwards usually by marrying Highland heiresses. The Frasers, who are alleged to take their name from the French *fraise* or strawberry-leaves of a ducal coronet, implying descent from the Dukes of Normandy — presumably illegitimate — became Sheriffs of Tweeddale, and settled at Oliver, also in Peebles-shire, further up Tweed. Then a scion of the house moved down to Neidpath and choosing a fine defensive site overhanging the river, started a new line.

Most famous of this branch was the patriot, Sir Simon Fraser, a great warrior of the Wars of Independence. For so notable a hero he started off his career in rather odd fashion. As a young man he fought against Edward I of England at the disastrous Battle of Dunbar, in 1296. He was captured and carried prisoner to England. There he accepted a parole situation and fought for Edward in France, learning his soldiering under that very expert if utterly ruthless master, as what was called a knight banneret. We learn that he earned four shillings a day for this service. With Edward having all but conquered Scotland, the English King restored to Sir Simon his lands in Peebles-shire, gave him a specially fine horse and even made him Keeper of the Forest of Traquair.

However, William Wallace arose to teach Scotland nationhood in the face of adversity, and what patriotism meant; and young Sir Simon saw the light. He left Edward's service, actually departing with the horses and armour of Sir William Durham, one of Edward's leaders, at the Siege of Caerlaverock in 1300, and went to join Wallace. This was before Robert Bruce did the same.

And now they were hard and fierce days for Fraser indeed, like the other fighters for freedom and independence. But Sir Simon came well out of it, becoming one of the most successful of the Scots commanders. In 1303, with Sir John Comyn, he defeated the English forces three times in one day, at the Battles of Roslin Muir. But he and Wallace were themselves defeated at Happrew,

not far from Neidpath, later the same year. In fury
Edward's troops devastated his lands. Sir Simon supported Bruce on Wallace's execution, joining him just
after his coronation. He distinguished himself at the disastrous Battle of Methven, when the new King suffered
his first defeat, was captured thereafter and taken to
London, where Edward wreaked his worst vengeance
upon him, hanging him naked, cutting him down while
still alive, disembowelling him and burning his entrails
before him, then hacking off his limbs before his head.
His head was then exposed on a spike on London Bridge,
beside that of Wallace, who had suffered the same
appalling fate. This was the price of patriotism, where
Edward Plantagenet was concerned.

It is unlikely that the present Neidpath included much
work of Sir Simon's time. He left only a daughter, who
married Hay of Yester and carried the property to that
family. It was the Hays who built the castle as it now

stands. They too were a spirited lot. The second Lord Hay fell at Flodden. The fifth was taken prisoner at the Battle of Pinkie, and sent south to the Tower of London, where he remained captive for long. Later he became one of Mary Oueen of Scots' most loyal supporters, but strongly objected to her marriage to Darnley. She would have been wise to have followed Hay's advice. Mary stayed a night at Neidpath in 1563; and her son, James VI, was here in 1587, holding a Privy Council in the castle. The eighth Lord was created Earl of Tweeddale in 1646, and commanded a royal regiment for Charles I. Neidpath was in consequence besieged in 1650 by Cromwell, on his expedition into Scotland and, unable to withstand his heavy cannon, like Borthwick, Tantallon, Dirleton and other Scottish castles, yielded. But at least the young Lord Hay, Tweeddale's son, held out longer than any other fortalice south of Forth.

The estate was purchased towards the end of that dramatic 17th century by William Douglas, first Duke of Queensberry, for his second son, the Earl of March, from whom is descended the present Earl of Wemyss and March. Sir Walter Scott spent cheerful days within Neidpath's ten-foot-thick walls when it was tenanted by Adam Ferguson the historian.

Newark Castle and the
Sorrowing Duchess

Here is one of the most romantic of all the Border land strongholds, situated in the Yarrow valley some five miles west of Selkirk and easily visible from the main A708 road, on its high mound above the steep banks of the river, within what is now the Duke of Buccleuch's Bowhill estate, a strong defensive position. It dates from the early 15th century, replacing an 'Auld Wark' of which no trace now remains. Its walls reach a thickness of ten feet, and although its roof has gone, it is still fairly complete to the wallhead. Formerly it was surrounded by the usual barmekin or curtain-walled court yard, with gatehouse.

Newark inevitably featured largely in Border history, with feuding and reiving rampant and English invaders a constant threat. It started as a royal hunting-seat, for the Ettrick Forest, of which Yarrow's valleys are part, was much favoured by the Scots Kings for sport, despite its reputation for sheltering outlaws and desperate fugitives. A panel bearing the royal arms still enhances the west walling. Although originally held by the Douglases, the Scotts of Buccleuch became hereditary keepers of the Forest, and Newark, and their Chief, the Duke, still owns the castle and much of the vast lands.

Newark's stirring history would take volumes to recount. Lord Grey and an English host assailed it in 1547, without success, but returned the following year and managed to gain entry, to burn it. Over 100 royalist captives including women camp-followers, were massacred in its courtyard after the disastrous defeat of Philiphaugh nearby in 1645, when the Covenanting general, David Leslie routed a smaller army of the great Marquis of Montrose in a ten-to-one struggle, a sorry outcome after all the latter's astonishing series of victories, Leslie egged on to these barbarous reprisals by the extremist Covenanting clergy accompanying his army. And five years later Newark was occupied by Cromwell's troops, after the Battle of Dunbar.

But undoubtedly the most dramatic story of this castle relates to Anne Scott. She was the heiress of Francis, second Earl of Buccleuch, whose only son died in infancy and so, on her father's and sister's decease, became Countess of Buccleuch in her own right. And in 1663 she married James Stewart, sometimes called Crofts, son of Charles II, and they were together created Duke and Duchess of Buccleuch and Monmouth.

This James was, of course, the controversial leader of the Monmouth Rising of 1685. He was alleged to be illegitimate, born to Charles when Prince of Wales in exile at The Hague during the Cromwellian regime, the

mother being Lucy Walters, the daughter of a Welsh squire in the royal entourage. The prince fell in love with Lucy. This amour greatly worried and incensed his mother, Queen Henrietta Maria, who had been arranging a marriage for him with the Princess Catherine of Braganza. She hurried to The Hague from Versaillies where she was exiled while her husband Charles I was in prison awaiting execution by Cromwell — her brother was the King of France. Charles, Prince of Wales, was in receipt of a pension from the French King, his uncle, and Henrietta Maria threatened her son that this would be cut off if he did not repudiate Lucy Walters and her baby. Charles Stewart was no very strong character, and he supinely accepted his mother's edict, and her command that he marry Catherine of Braganza. This he did, although the marriage was in fact unlawful, for the prince had had a secret marriage to Lucy. But once wed to the Portuguese princess and succeeding his decapitated father on the United Kingdom throne, the new King felt that he could not disown the queen; so his son James, by Lucy, was accepted as illegitimate, although he was not, his father's marriage-lines remaining as evidence for long. All efforts to persuade Charles to nominate the protestant James as his heir were unavailing — although he was said to be fond of his son — for the King was a secret Roman Catholic, and he was determined that his Catholic brother, James, Duke of York, should succeed him; which he in due course did, as James VII and II, for a disastrous four years before fleeing over seas.

James, the nephew, Duke of Buccleuch and Monmouth, then led the Protestant revolt, but with utterly inadequate resources and a tiny force. He was defeated at the Battle of Sedgemoor in 1685, captured, and executed by his uncle, King James. But by his duchess, Anne Scott, he left two sons, one, Earl of Doncaster, dying young, but the other, Earl of Dalkeith, producing four sons, the eldest of which in due course succeeded his grandmother as Duke of Buccleuch, the

Monmouth title having been forfeited on his grand-father's execution. So the present Duke of Buccleuch, in direct male descent, could lawfully claim the name of Stewart instead of Montague-Douglas-Scott, with all that that could entail.

Anne, the sorrowing Duchess, returned to Newark Castle to end her days there. And Newark, Sir Walter Scott made the scene of his *Lay of the The Last Minstrel*.

> *He passed where Newark's stately tower*
> *Looked out from Yarrow's birchen bower;*
> *The minstrel gazed with wishful eye*
> *No humbler resting-place was nigh.*
> *With hesitating step at last,*
> *The embattled portal arch he passed*
> *The Duchess marked his weary pace*
> *His timid mein and reverent face,*
> *And bade her page the menials tell*
> *That they should tend the old man well*
> *For she had known adversity*
> *Though born in such a high degree*
> *In pride of power, in beauty's bloom*
> *Had wept o'er Monmoth's bloody tomb!*

Orchardton Tower and the French Connection

Orchardton is unique, the only circular peel-tower in the land. There are plenty of round towers to keeps and castles; but here the free-standing keep itself is circular, although there was formerly a courtyard, square enough, with curtain-walls on all sides but the north, within which were subsidiary outbuildings, vaulted and substantial. What moved its builder to erect his fortalice thus, much more difficult architecturally, is not recorded. No doubt he had to put up with considerable scoff and jeer while he was doing it, too.

The building, now in the care of Historic Scotland, stands in a secluded Galloway valley some four miles south of Dalbeattie and not far from the head of Orchardton Bay. Its walls are eight feet thick at the lower storeys, narrowing somewhat as they rise to the fourth storey and the parapet with wall-walk, the rooms above basement level being circular. The tower is now roofless but there would be the usual garret storey above parapet-level, where there is still the attractive little gabled cap-house, giving access from the turnpike stairway in the thickness of the walling to the parapet-walk. Originally the entrance was at first-floor level, reached by the usual removable timber-stair for security reasons.

These lands came to a rather noteworthy character in the early 15th century, one Alexander de Carnys, or Cairns, Provost of Lincluden College, and a supporter of

the mighty house of Douglas — Lincluden, also in the Stewartry of Kirkcudbright, being a Douglas foundation. Alexander was a noted churchman, and was chosen, in 1412, during the regency of the Duke of Albany for the captive young James I, to be one of three special envoys to go to France on a diplomatic mission, for which £200 was advanced for expenses — so it must have been an important mission, for £200 was a great deal of money in those days, and Robert, Duke of Albany, not notable for extravagance.

Anyway, there was delay after delay in the mission setting out, and in fact it never got to France. Nevertheless, the money gradually disappeared — and Provost Alexander Cairns was generally esteemed as responsible. Certainly the Scots Treasury never got it back. It is amusing to speculate that this unique round Tower of Orchardton may have been built with the missing £200. We know that the tower was completed in 1456 by John Cairns, probably the illegitimate son of the Provost — who, of course, as a churchman, was forbidden to marry.

A grandson of this John was implicated, with Gordon of Lochinvar, a kinsman, in the murder of Maclellan of

Bombie, hereditary sheriff of the Stewartry for the Crown. Maclellan, Chief of that powerful Galloway clan, was slain within the open doorway of St. Giles High Kirk in Edinburgh in 1527 — which location seems to have caused more offence to the citizenry than the death itself. The Douglas Earl of Angus was then ruling Scotland for the young James V, appointing his uncle Archibald Douglas, Provost of Edinburgh. And under this chief magistrate's protection the assassins of Maclellan 'walked the streets with impunity even though the Queen herself deemed it necessary to have Douglas's safe-conduct to walk abroad.'

But probably Orchardton's most appealing story dates from a much later period. By Jacobite times the property had been purchased by a branch of the great family of Maxwell; and the grandson and heir of Sir Robert Maxwell of Orchardton was one of those involved in Prince Charles Edward's cause. He distinguished himself by managing to escape from the Jacobite force besieged in Carlisle by Cumberland, along with a Colonel Brown, of the French Garde Ecossais, and rejoining the Prince in Scotland not long before Culloden. Here he was attached to the Prince's staff. However, after the fatal battle, Captain Maxwell was captured and returned to Carlisle, along with so many others, for trial for treason. He appears to have thought that the fact that he had been an officer in the service of the King of France would tell against him, and this being recorded in his papers, in his cell at Carlisle Castle he sought to destroy the evidence by eating his papers. He was caught in the act, however, and the papers were taken and handed over to the magistrate who was to try him. Either this individual was kinder of heart than most of his sort or else he was just sickened by condemning young men to be hanged for their loyalty to the Stewarts, for he ruled that these papers proved that Captain Maxwell was not just one more rebel in arms against King George but was an offi-cer in the army of King Louis XV of France, and therefore had to be treated as a legitimate prisoner-of-war. He should be returned to France, to be dealt with by the military authorities there.

This was duly done, and in France the young man suffered no penalty, since the French, of course, favoured the Stewart cause. It is good to relate that, in course of time, with the Jacobite cause more or less moribund and the scars healing, Maxwell was permitted to return to Galloway and take his place as Laird of Orchardton, a happier outcome than for most of his colleagues.

Pitcaple Castle and the Great Marquis

Central Aberdeenshire is particularly rich in castles, as in much else, a large and fascinating land insufficiently appreciated by much of the rest of Scotland. Partly, probably, because of the farmlands and pastures being so rich, partly because of the lack of major industrial developments and partly because this area was remote from the Border wars and did not have to suffer more than local warfare, the castles have survived better than elsewhere. Not that they were without their excitements, but these did not usually involve demolition or burning down.

Pitcaple is a fine house, standing on the River Urie about five miles north-west of Inverurie. In 1457, James II confirmed a charter of Pitcaple to David, son of Sir William Leslie, fourth of Balquhain, a powerful family in these parts, who had got Balquhain from David II as early as 1340. Nothing visible of the present castle belongs to this early period, but there are traces of older work incorporated in the building, and we know that it used to be surrounded by a moat, with drawbridge, curtain-walls and gatehouse. Today it looks a fairly typical early 17th century fortalice on the Z-plan — that is, a tall main-block with circular towers projecting at the north-east and south-west angles; typical, that is, save for the roofs of the towers and turrets, which are odd in that they are concave in shape instead of the usual conical.

157

This is since 1830 when one of the lairds went on a tour of France and came back smitten with the idea of making Pitcaple's roofs look like the French ones.

Considering its situation, Pitcaple has been the scene of quite a number of events of national significance. James IV came here, no doubt on his way to and from St. Duthac's at Tain, where he was wont to go on pilgrimage, via Darnaway Castle in Moray and his mistress Flaming Janet Kennedy — as recounted under Cassillis House. His grand-daughter, Mary Queen of Scots, also visited, when she came north in 1562 to put down the power of the Gordons, at the Battle of Corrichie, at which Huntly himself died and his son was executed. The Queen actually spent the night at Balquhain, two miles to the south, but oddly enough came on to Pitcaple for breakfast, staying long enough to plant a thorn-tree. This survived until 1856. It is now replaced by a red maple planted by a later Queen Mary, in 1923.

The first Mary's great-grandson, Charles II was also at Pitcaple, spending a night here in July 1650, after his landing at Garmouth in Moray from his exile in Holland. He is reputed to have danced under the aforementioned thorn-tree. It is good that the young King felt like dancing on this occasion, for this was not a happy interlude in his life, and he never forgave the Scots for forcing concessions from him in exchange for promises of support. His room on the second floor is still known as the King's Room.

But the most dramatic incident in Pitcaple's long story was probably that of only two months earlier when, after his betrayal by Macleod of Assynt, the great Montrose was brought here on his grim way south to execution at Edinburgh, preceded by a herald crying 'Here comes James Graham, a traitor to his country!' The King's Viceroy, we read, was 'seated upon a little shelty horse, with out a saddle, but a quilt of rags and straw, and pieces of rope for stirrups, his feet fastened under the horse's belly, with a tether and a bit halter for a bridle.'

The laird, John Leslie, was himself a supporter of King Charles, but absent at the time, and his wife was in fact a kinswoman of the Marquis. Which makes it the more ironical that his principal captor was General David Leslie, victor of the Battle of Philiphaugh and later Lord Newark.

Lady Pitcaple was a woman of spirit and played a subtle game, not on the face of it objecting to the Marquis's ill-treatment and his immuring in a vaulted cellar of the castle, but feasting and wining General Leslie and his officers in especially lavish fashion. And not only the officers, for she sent downstairs to Montrose's immediate guards a sufficiency of whisky to put them all 'into a state of temulent beatitude', caring little what happened to their prisoner. Late in the night she came down in person to the cellar, to find the Marquis the only man awake. She told him that if he followed her she could bring him to an underground passage, opening from a contiguous vault, which would bring him out beyond the courtyard's curtain-wall and moat. She could not loose his bonds, but he ought to be able to hobble down to the riverside and get away.

The prisoner thanked her warmly — but refused. 'Whether or not I escaped this, in my person,' he told her, 'I would never escape in my mind and conscience. And I have reached such stage where my peace of mind is worth more than all else to me. Too many have already suffered and died on my account. Kin of my own in especial. You are that. There would be no mercy for you. Being a woman would not save you from Argyll's spleen. Moreover, your husband is already in bad odour with the Covenanters, over the Engagement trouble. My escape from his house could put a halter round his neck. I thank you — but no!' Nothing the lady could say would shake his resolution. Montrose was marched south in the morning.

As well as these national affairs, Pitcaple saw many more local excitements, for the Leslies were a wild lot. The fourth laird killed George Leith of Freefield in a brawl and in consequence his family was at feud with the Leiths; he was eventually forced to leave the country and died a captain in the army of the Emperor. In 1630 James Leslie, second son of the laird, was involved in the terrible tragedy of the burning of Frendraught, when in consequence of another feud with Crichton of Frendraught, that castle was set alight, with the help of gunpowder, and Viscount Aboyne, son of Huntly, and five others were burned to death. The laird himself, the same who was absent when Montrose was at Pitcaple, and who entertained Charles II, died in 1651 at the Battle of Worcester, fighting for the King. He had even bought up all the claret in the neighbourhood to feast — possibly something to do with that dancing under the thorn-tree.

Despite all this, the Leslies retained possession of Pitcaple until 1757 when Sir James died, and his half-sister carried the property to her husband, one of the Lumsdens of Cushnie, with whose descendants it still remains.

Pitreavie Castle and the Curse

The name Pitreavie is familiar to most of us in Scotland as the source of weather-bulletins, being the joint Royal Naval and Royal Air Force meteorological centre in West Fife; and as such tends to make its own impact on our lives and plans. Probably, however, few realise that Pitreavie has been making an impact of a different kind for a long time, since the beginning of the 18th century in fact — as will appear.

The castle itself, although now a Ministry of Defence establishment, enlarged and surrounded by its subsidiary buildings and hutments, is still intact, an early 17th-century fortified house of some size and character. It was built around 1615 by Sir Henry Wardlaw, a member of a prominent and ancient Fothrif family, one of whom, Walter de Wardlaw, had been Bishop of Glasgow in 1368 and became Scotland's first cardinal; and his nephew, Henry, Bishop of St. Andrews and founder of Scotland's first university in 1411. Pitreavie's builder was the son of Sir Cuthbert Wardlaw of Balmule, at the other side of Dunfermline. He was made Chamberlain to Anne of Denmark, James VI's queen, whose marriage-jointure from her husband was Dunfermline Abbey, Palace and lands. Pitreavie lies only three miles south-east of Dunfermline and would be part of the abbey lands, which came his way. Made Warden of the palace and territories, he did rather well out of it, was knighted in 1613 by King James and made one of the new Nova Scotia baronets in 1631 by King Charles. Pitreavie Castle was to be the suitable domicile for such a well-doing character and a long line of worthy successors.

Alas, it was not to be — not as far as the castle is concerned, at any rate, although the present Wardlaw baronet, in far-away New Zealand, is the 21st. Fairly soon after gaining his baronetcy Sir Cuthbert died; and in 1651 the Battle of Inverkeithing was fought not far away, when Cromwell and 6,000 of his Ironsides defeated with great slaughter 4,000 Scots fighting for Charles II, 1,600 being slain and 1,200 taken prisoner. Of the remaining 1,200, a party of Clan Maclean, fleeing westwards for their own country, came upon Pitreavie Castle and besought temporary refuge there. But Sir Henry's son, the second baronet, would have none of them, cursing them as wild Catholic hielantmen, he and his servants driving the Macleans off by hurling stone-slates at them from the roof. However, Highlanders have their own variety of cursing, possibly more effective than the Fife sort, with second-sight and the like involved; and these cursed back, asserting that he and his would not long remain lairds of this Pitreavie.

I have not ascertained exactly how long it took for the

Macleans' curse to work. But the laird died in just over a year, and his son, a third Sir Henry passed away without heir a year after his father. The lands passed to another branch of the family and were sold.

In 1696, the sixth baronet of Pitreavie, but no longer possessing the property, married Elizabeth Halkett of Pitfirrane, daughter of a neighbouring laird; and it was to this lady that I was referring when I said that Pitreavie had been making an impact on many of us for some time. For she was a highiy talented creature, admitted author of the pseudo-archaic ballad *Hardycanute*. But what is more important, she is now believed to have been also the author of sundry much better-known Scots ballads which have generally been considered to be authentic and traditional, such as *Sir Patrick Spens* and *The Bonnie Earl o'Moray*, possibly even *The Queen's Four Maries*. I have long had an interest in these ballads and have been uncomfortably aware that they tended to be not quite all that they seemed and have been accepted to be. Many of the historical details were quite wrong, for instance — some of the geography too, some wildly out, although generations have gone on revering them and singing them with great emotion. *Sir Patrick Spens* is particularly full of chronological impossibilities; and *The Bonnie Earl o' Moray* also barely makes sense when you look into it, however excellent as a stirring song. And none of the Queen's famous four Maries suffered execution.

Now, however, we can see the reason for this. These ballads were written by a brilliant song-writer, at a comparatively late date, possibly based on traditional handed-down legends — but Lady Wardlaw of Pitreavie did not know much history. She, undoubtedly, would have been the first to admit this, for she was a most modest woman and produced her ballads anony-mously. Probably she would have been highly sur-prised to learn of their enduring popularity and accep-tance.

It is all comparatively easy to see the point once it has

been made evident; we are all good at that. For instance:

O lang will his lady,
Look owre the Castle Doune
Ere she see the Earl o'Moray
Come sounding through the toun.

and

O lang, lang may the ladies sit,
Wi' their fans into their hands,
Ere they see Sir Patrick Spens
Come sailing to the strand.

and

The Queen looked owre the castle wa',
Beheld baith dale and down,
And then she saw Young Waters
Come riding into town.

Three verses from three different ballads. Oh, Elizabeth!

Provan Hall and
a King's Conscience

This small but very interesting and unspoiled fortalice, now in the care of the National Trust for Scotland, should be better-known. It stands amidst the built-up and industrialised area of Glasgow's suburb of Baillieston, in what is now Auchinlea Park — indeed this is where Baillieston gets its name. Provan Hall was the property of Holy Church until the Reformation, and it was the country residence of the Prebendary of St Nicholas and Canon of Barlanark, one of the dignitaries of Glasgow Cathedral — whose town residence, incidentally, was Provands Lordship, reputed to be the oldest house in Glasgow, which was part of St Nicholas Hospice. At the Reformation, when the Church lands were parcelled out, this property came to Sir William Baillie. The Baillies were descended from the great house of Balliol, of which King John Balliol, of course, is the most famous, or notorious. His mother was the renowned Devorgilla, heiress of the ancient Lords of Galloway, who founded Balliol College, Oxford in memory of her husband, as well as Sweetheart Abbey in Kirkcudbrightshire.

The buildings of Provan Hall no doubt existed before Baillie's time, but seemingly he altered and adapted them considerably so that the house looks fairly typical of the later 16th century, whereas it is somewhat earlier. It still retains its early plan of a courtyard-house, however, with the original buildings on the north side, a later dwelling-house superseding the stabling and other domestic out-buildings of the south side, and high curtain-walls sealing both ends, that to the east having the handsome gateway, arched and moulded, with a little gatehouse chamber above, and all guarded by a typical late-16th century shothole. The fortalice is unusual in being only two storeys high. The basement is vaulted in three chambers, notable in that the kitchen with great fireplace, oven and slopdrain, has its vaulting running east and west, while the other two cellars have it north and south. There is a stairtower projecting at the northeast corner, but the turnpike stair has been removed and replaced by an outside straight forestair in the courtyard.

There must be many stories to be told about Provan Hall; but my favourite relates to that interesting and so very human monarch, James IV. For, odd as it may sound, this was his house for a time, for the King himself became the Prebendary of Barlanark and Canon of Glasgow.

It happened this way. Young James, Duke of Rothesay, aged 15 or so, was estranged from his distinctly difficult father James III, and was used by the resurgent nobles as a sort of puppet against the weak King. This all culmi-

nated, in 1488, in the Battle of Sauchieburn, at which the rebel lords, with young James of Rothesay, as figurehead, defeated his father's forces. The King ignominiously fled the field before the end of the battle, but was thrown by his bolting horse at the Mill of the Bannockburn. He was carried into a stable there, unrecognised, by the miller. Believing himself to be dying, he called for a priest to shrive him. The miller went out and beseeched some horsemen who rode up to go find a priest; but these were some of the rebel lords, on the monarch's trail. One of them, the grim Lord Gray, declared that he would shrive the King, and going into the stable he stabbed the monarch to death.

Presently young James was brought to the scene and was shown his dead father, the lords pointing out that he was now the King. At the sight and realisation the youth was shattered, perceiving at last the sort of men who were using him and now had him in their power, and recognising something of his own responsibility for his father's death. He vowed there and then, in the stable, never to forget his blood-guiltiness, but also to try to make a better King than his unhappy sire. In token of which he took down a length of harness-chain which was hanging from a peg on the walling, and tied this around his waist and loins, next to the skin, to be worn as an uncomfortable reminder of his guilt and his vow, promising never to remove it. And wear it he did, even though this has often been dismissed as a mere legend, for in later life the Lord High Treasurer's Accounts show recurring items 'to ane link to the King's chain, so much' — indication of James's increasing girth around the middle. Indeed the superstitious imputed the eventual terrible defeat of Flodden to the fact that, in James's 'dallying' at Ford Castle with Lady Heron before the battle, while waiting for the English army to come up, he put aside the chain — presumably the lady found it uncomfortable — and when his body was recovered after the battle there was no chain thereon.

Be that as it may, this chain-wearing was not enough for the conscience-stricken young monarch, for as part of his penance he had himself appointed Prebendary of Barlanark and Canon — although there is no suggestion that he took holy orders. As Canon he took practical steps for the advancement of his chosen church, for he it was, in the very first year of his reign 'concludit and ordainit ... that for the honour and public gud of the realme the sege (see) of Glasgow be erectit in ane Archbishoprick with sic previlegis as accordis of law and siclick as the Archbishoprick of York has in all dignities, emunities and previlegis', and so petitioned Pope Alexander VI. Later the King renewed and extended the privileges and exemptions and the jurisdictions of the archbishop, and initiated improvements of the cathedral itself. James's piety, of course, was always of the highly practical sort, as witness his later pilgrimages to Whithorn and Tain, which could be combined with visits to his mistress, as related under Cassillis House.

Rossend Castle
and Poet's Licence

Standing high above the Fife town of Burntisland, yet within the burgh, Rossend Castle, proud, fair and white, looks as though nothing could ever disturb its centuries-old assurance and serenity. Yet only a few years ago it was not only a derelict ruin but under long-standing threat of demolition. Rossend — actually the name should be Burntisland Castle, and always was until one Matthew Campbell from Skye bought it and changed its name for some reason in the late 18th century — was a sad story of municipal neglect and worse than neglect; for Burntisland Town Council purchased it, early this century, to use its land for council housing, and finding

no use for the castle itself allowed it to stand empty, deteriorate and become vandalised. When the Council wanted to pull it down, as an eyesore, a number of us stepped in to try to save it. A long battle ensued, the town intent on demolition, one Provost declaring that it was 'merely a monument to outdated landlordism' — and the would-be preservers using every device possible to halt such a fate.

Unfortunately Rossend was a big place, and being set now in the middle of a housing-scheme, was not attractive to most possible restorers as a home. Things got worse, the Council called in the Army to blow it up, the Army refused, but matters looked desperate when sundry architects evolved a scheme whereby the place might be restored, not as a house or museum but as offices for architectural staff. Thanks to their efforts, and the courage and drive of one in particular, Rossend is now saved for the foreseeable future, a centre of great interest and attraction, a hive of industry of a sort and something of which Burntisland should be proud indeed — although not its municipal representatives.

Its earlier story is a fascinating one. It was built by one Peter Durie, of an old Fife family, whose father was Abbot of Dunfermline, then the richest abbey in the land and this territory Dunfermline property — this in the early 16th century. It passed into Melville hands, and the laird was Sir Robert Melville of Murdocairnie, one of Mary Queen of Scots' staunchest supporters, when the Queen herself came here in 1563. She was on her way to St Andrews and spent the night at Burntisland after the Forth crossing. And here, in a room still pointed out as Mary's bedchamber, the French courtier and poet, Chastelard secreted himself under the royal bed to await the Queen's retiral — for, like many another of her court he was hopelessly in love with the fascinating Mary. Whether he sneezed or coughed or left a foot sticking out is not reported, but the wretched poet was discovered and dragged forth, causing the Queen to call in alarm for help. He would have been despatched there and then by the royal guards, for apparently this was not his first attempt on the Queen's person; but Mary's half-brother, the cool and calculating James Stewart, Earl of Moray, took charge and declared that Chastelard should be kept close confined, taken with them to St Andrews, and there properly tried for lese-majesty, offence against the monarch's person. And at St Andrews, thereafter, he was duly executed, as the law prescribed, his last words being:

'Adieu, thou most beautiful and most cruel princess in the world!'

Queen Mary's personal reaction to this is not recorded.

The famous Kirkcaldy of Grange held the castle for a time thereafter, but in 1666 the property was acquired by Sir James Wemyss of Caskieberry, who was created Lord Burntisland for life on marrying his kinswoman the Countess of Wemyss in her own right. Exciting days, for the very next year a fleet of 30 Dutch ships arrived in the Forth, and opened fire on castle and town. Sundry privateers in Burntisland harbour dragged their cannon ashore and up the hill and opened return fire. Presumably this was sufficient to drive off the Dutch, for the only damage reported was a few chimneys knocked over.

About 50 years later, in 1715, the castle was held by the Earl of Mar's Jacobite forces and it made the headquarters of the redoubtable Rob Roy MacGregor for his campaign in Fife.

I wonder whether the architectural draughtsmen sometimes let their minds wander as they calculate and draw?

Stewarthall and
the Judge's Lady

The level floodlands of the Forth near Stirling are perhaps the most significant area in all Scotland. For here it was that the great battles of our history were fought — Bannockburn, Stirling Bridge, Sauchieburn, the two Battles of Falkirk as well as many lesser struggles — for the sufficient reason that here was the first place where invading armies might cross the barrier of the Forth estuary — and be held up by smaller forces using the mud-flats, pools and burns of the flood-plain to aid them, Scotland's moat, as it were. So any castles and fortalices sited in these wetlands were apt to experience stirring times, to have a grandstand view of history in the making, if not to take part in it.

Stewarthall arrived too late on the scene to have any part in those early battles; but warfare in Scotland continued until much later dates than in many lands, what with the Montrose, Covenant, Cromwellian and Jacobite campaigns, and battles were still being fought hereabouts as late as 1746. So Stewarthall did not altogether escape excitements. This is a comparatively late name, for the property formerly was called Wester Polmaise. The house stands on the flats of the Bannock Burn itself, half-a-mile from its confluence with the Forth, a mile north-west of the mining village of Fallin and three miles east of Stirling, surprisingly remote-seeming considering its central site. The building is a little unusual, consisting

of a tall, white-washed tower of four storeys with a slender stair-turret at one angle, but no parapet or wall-walk. The roof-level apparently has been altered, however, probably in the 17th century, so that the original work would be earlier and may have been more conventional. A lower addition has been built to the east probably in the 18th century. The original doorway was in the west front, now built up, and inserted here is a panel bearing the arms of the Stirling family with those of Hamilton, the initials A.S. and A.H. and the motto GANG FORWARD.

Sir Alexander Stirling of Garden, a Court of Session judge, succeeded to Wester Polmaise on the death of his sister, widow of Alexander Cowane, a Stirling surgeon, presumably kin to the 17th-century founder of Cowane's Hospital there. The Stirlings were Jacobites. Indeed Stirling of Garden, father of the above, was brought to trial for high treason in 1708, but acquitted for lack of evidence. However, the story I have for Stewarthall concerns another judge, likewise with Jacobite sympathies, the Hon. James Erskine, Lord Grange, brother of the sixth Earl of Mar, 'Bobbing John' the commander of the Jacobite forces of 1715. He was for a time Lord Justice Clerk before being deprived. He took his judicial title of Grange from the house of Prestongrange, near Prestonpans. He led a very colourful life for a Lord of Session. His diary, for instance under 10 June 1718 reads: 'I drank and whor'd and followed sensual pleasures, but I never gave over reading, tho' my lewdness hinder'd exceedingly my proffitting at any study.' Yet, another entry the same year records his studying Hebrew every morning at 7 o'clock under a university professor.

Well, Lord Grange had a difficult wife. He had married the beautiful but violent-tempered Rachel Chiesly, daughter of the notorious John Chiesly, Laird of Dalry and Gorgie, who was hanged for the assassination of Lockhart of Carnwath, Lord President of the Court of Session. So she came of impetuous stock. Lady Grange, at any rate, appears to have made her husband's life less pleasant than he would have liked. Not only did she take exception to his infidelities but she accused him of Jacobitism — much more serious — and threatened to go to London to inform on him there 'for high treason and other capital crimes'. She had left Prestongrange and taken a lodging near her husband's Edinburgh quarters, where she used to abuse him in the street in noisy demonstrations. According to his lordship 'she cried and raged against me ... chased me from place to place in the most indecent and shameless manner and threatened to attack me on the Bench.'

This could not go on, of course, and Lord Grange hatched a project with his friend, the famous or notorious Simon Fraser, Lord Lovat. The lady was to be kidnapped one night by Lovat's Highland servants, on the eve of her departure for London to inform on her spouse, and conveyed elsewhere. She was taken, bundled into a sedan chair in the street, seated there upon the knees of one Mr Foster of Carsebonny, although according to her own later account she fought valiantly for freedom to 'the detriment of her skin, hair and teeth.' This was in 1732.

The abductors carried Lady Grange to Wester Polmaise 'the house belonging to a Stewart, where Lovat conferred with her gaoler as to her future custody.' So this must have been the character who changed the fort-alice's name to Stewarthall. I have been unable to discover anything more about this shadowy figure. But an interesting glimpse of conditions prevailing reveals that Lady Grange must have been detailed here for some time, for an attempt was made to rescue her, and by no less than the sons of Rob Roy MacGregor — who died two years later — and who, we are told 'nearly succeeded in rescuing the unhappy lady Grange from her captors, for the sake of the reward.' So her abduction must have been rather less secret than hoped for. And who was offering the reward?

At any rate the attempt failed, and the judge's wife was taken north into the Highlands and eventually, of all places, she was immured on the distant Isle of St Kilda where she would surely be far enough away to ensure Lord Grange's peace, he now being 60 but notably active in various ways, plunging openly into politics, despite his seat on the Bench, as well as more personal ploys. There seems to have been remarkably little fuss about the lady's disappearance, the general assumption being that she had indeed gone to London, where of course anything might happen.

Eight years later, however, Lady Grange managed to get a letter smuggled from St Kilda to the Lord Advocate — who was no friend of Grange's — telling him that she was held captive in 'that vile, nasty, stinking poor isle,' so she had not lost all her eloquence. She added that her captors treated her with great harshness but admitted that they allowed her an anker (eight and a half imperial gallons) of spirits annually — presumably in the hope of her drinking herself to death.

The Lord Advocate made something of a fuss about this, and the lady was hastily removed first to Assynt in Sutherland and then to Skye, where in May 1745, after 13 years imprisonment, she died. She was buried at Dunvegan. Lord Grange wrote a letter of thanks to Lord Lovat, with payment for board and funeral expenses, 'for the timely death of that person. Her retaining wit and facetiousness to the last surprises me.'

Grange fell on evil days, even being glad to accept a loan of two guineas from a fellow-Scot in London in 1748, and died in 1754, aged 75. Simon, Lord Lovat, of course, did even less well, having his head chopped off at Tower Hill, for his peculiar share in the Forty-Five rising.

Threave Castle and Mons Meg

The great family of Douglas all but ruled Scotland for long, more powerful in men and means and spirit than the royal Stewarts, and allied to them by marriage generation after generation. Douglas Castle in Lanarkshire was their original home, but from the late 14th century Threave, two miles from Castle Douglas in Galloway, was their main stronghold. Inevitably, with such ownershlp, Threave is a mine of stories and incidents.

It was built soon after 1369 by Archibald the Grim, who succeeded as third Earl of Douglas, illegitimate son of the Good Sir James, Bruce's great friend, who died taking the dead king's heart on crusade and seems never to have married. Threave is set on an island in the River Dee, a huge and massive keep, walls eight feet thick and honeycombed with mural chambers, its flush parapet and walk 70 feet above ground. Security was obviously all-important to its builder, for there was no bridge to the island, although almost certainly there would be a zigzag underwater causeway; and the entrance to the keep was at first-floor level, reached by a removable timber bridge from the gatehouse in the curtain-wall. Access to the gatehouse had to be by boat, otherwise — which must have meant that all the great domestic appendages of a powerful lord's household, stables, byres, barns and the rest, were on the main river bank — inconvenient one would have thought. The feeling is that Archibald the Grim must have had an uneasy conscience. But then

Forward! was the Douglas motto, or in its French form, *Jamais Arriere* — not Love or Trust Thy Neighbour!

Archibald's son, the fourth Earl, and also Duke of Touraine, married the Princess Margaret, sister of James I, whose two sons died at the infamous Black Dinner in Edinburgh Castle in 1440, leaving Threave and the mighty Lordship of Galloway, although not the earldom, to be inherited by their sister Margaret, the renowned Fair Maid of Galloway. She may have been fair in her looks, as in the size of her inheritance, but there seems to have been some doubts about her morals locally — although, to be sure, we are in no position to judge at this remove in time, and besides, heiresses were apt to have a difficult time of it. At any rate she eventually married her cousin William, who became eighth Earl, and so kept the lands in the family. He it was who was reputed to have kept a retinue of 1,000 armed men at Threave.

The castle was the scene of a notorious killing, which sparked off a train of circumstance which was to bring about the downfall of this Black Douglas line, out of which disaster the rival though related line of the Red

Douglases of Angus arose. This killing was the hanging of Sir Patrick Maclellan of Bombie, Chief of that powerful Galloway clan, and indeed Sheriff of Galloway. He was strung up by Douglas from the fatal Gallows knob, a granite block which still projects over the main gateway of the castle. There was no doubt sufficient reason for this act of feudal justice; but King James II seized on it as a good excuse to bring down the over-great power of the Douglas Earls, and an act of forfeiture was passed against Earl William. The Douglases scorned this, of course, and the scene was set for a show-down at Threave.

Mons Meg now comes into the picture, Scotland's most famous cannon, long the pride of Edinburgh Castle, with a dramatic story of its own. It has been assumed that this mighty piece of ordnance got its name from its supposed construction at Mons in Flanders. But almost certainly this is a mistake. When James II came in great force to Galloway to reduce Threave and the Douglases to submission, he was presented with this outsize piece of artillery by the wronged Maclelland — although why they should possess such a weapon is not explained. It had been forged at Kirkcudbright, the Maclellan 'capital', by a blacksmith called Brawny Kim of Mollance — Mollance lies less than five miles from Threave — and, who knows, the circumstances of the Maclellans making this cannon might have had something to do with the Earl of Douglas's need to hang Sir Patrick? Be that as it may, the artillery proved so successful at Threave that it got called thereafter Mollance Meg, after the smith's wife, by the grateful monarch, who also made Kirkcudbright a royal burgh on the strength of it. It is the local tradition that when Mollance Meg fired its first granite ball at the castle — reputed to weigh as much as a Galloway cow and to have required a peck of gunpowder per shot — it smashed its way right through the building and took off the hand of the Fair Maid as she sat at table with her lord and was raising a wine-cup to her lips — a nice indication both of the Douglas sang froid during a siege and of the gunner's accuracy. The non-Douglas Gallovidians used to maintain that this was a choice example of the vengeance of God in destroying the hand which had been given in wedlock to two brothers, and this even while the lawful spouse of the first was still alive. This might be slightly prejudiced. At any rate, this occasion marked not only the fall of Threave but the beginning of the end for the Black Douglases, and the start of Mollance or Mons Meg's fame. Earl William was shortly afterwards stabbed to death by the hand of King James himself at Stirling, although there under the monarch's safe-conduct, a dire story.

We read that, about 50 years later, James's grandson, James IV, had the cannon transferred from Edinburgh Castle to Holyrood for some national festivity, when the High Treasurer's accounts record the following charges:

To the menstrallis that playit b£foir Mons down the gait, fourteen shillings.
Eight elle of claith, to be Mons a claith to cover her, nine shillings and four pence.

After the Douglas fall, Threave Castle became a royal fortress, and formed part of the jointure, or marriage-settlement of successive queens. It was used as a gaol for French prisoners-of-war during the Napoleonic campaigns.

Tioram and the Great Frog

Perhaps few others fulfil the story-book ideals of a Highland Chief's stronghold as does Castle Tioram, set on a tidal islet in the narrow mouth of Loch Moidart in the extreme north of Argyll, amidst wooded hills. Dominating all in romantic isolation on the summit of its towering sea-girt rock, it was the principal seat of Clanranald; and although abandoned since the Jacobite Rising of 1715, its lofty keep and stern curtain-walls remain intact to their wallheads, a notable magnet for the more adventurous summer visitors.

Its story is a strange mixture of dramatic true history and picturesque legend, often hard to disentangle one from the other. Probably the first castle, the high, blank-walled enclosure which follows the irregular shape of the islet-top, was built by the great Somerled, King of Argyll and the first Lord of the Isles, progenitor of all Clan Donald, in the 12th century. It was added to by succeed-ing descendants, and Amy MacRuari of Garmoran, wife of John, seventh Lord of the Isles, erected the tall keep towards the end of the 14th century. Her husband had divorced her in order that he might marry Princess Margaret, daughter of Robert II, Bruce's grandson; and the wronged lady came here with her dispossessed family. From her second son, Ranald, springs the Clanranald division of the mighty Clan Donald. Thereafter, Castle Tioram was the centre and scene of continual turmoil, battle and excitement, both in clan and national affairs.

It is told of Alan of Garmoran, fifth of Clanranald, that when at sea he was approached by a much larger fleet of hostile Maclean galleys which he was unable to fight nor yet to escape. So he pretended to be dead, had his body laid out on the stern-platform under a draped plaid, his men allegedly mourning and conveying the corpse for burial on Iona. With suitable reverence for the dead the Macleans escorted him so far on his way; and when free of them at last, and Alan landed, it is recorded that he lit a number of bonfires on Maclean Mull land to celebrate his resurrection. Sadly, however, this resourceful individual was beheaded in 1509, not very long afterwards, at Blair Atholl in Perthshire, in the presence of James IV, What was he doing there is uncertain.

In 1554 Queen Mary of Guise, Mary Queen of Scots' mother, commanded Huntly and Argyll to assail Castle Tioram by land and sea, using artillery and all force. They besieged it for five weeks, unsuccessfully; then the wily Campbell withdrew his ships and seemed to sail for home disheartened, but crept back under cover of darkness, and landing his men, attacked and managed to take the castle by rushing his men over the tidal sands. A century later Oliver Cromwell's troops managed to capture and occupy the stronghold in rather better time, with more advanced weaponry. Several cannonballs were found lodged in the masonry during repairs in 1888, but from which of these assaults is uncertain.

Colourful, if murky, was the career of a descendant, John, twelfth Chief, who succeeded as Clanranald in 1670. He had fought, as a youth, in the Montrose campaigns, but seems to have been a nasty piece of work. He specialised, later in life, in shooting at anything which came within range of the topmost tower of Castle Tioram, with his gun which for some reason rejoiced in the name of The Cuckoo. On one occasion he shot and killed a man spied on the mainland shore, across the narrow sound, and who turned out to be one of his principal clansmen, coming to visit him. On another, missing some

money, he suspected his personal ghillie, another man and a girl servant of the theft, and incontinently hanged the two men out-of-hand. The girl he marooned on a tidal rock nearby to drown. A third example was when he hanged his woman cook for helping herself to her master's snuff — a rash female, surely.

However, in time, John's sins caught up with him, allegedly. He came to be haunted by a familiar spirit in the shape of a large black frog, which the local priest either could not or would not exorcise. This creature became the Chief's constant but unwelcome companion. Whenever he tried to escape, it followed him. When he left it sleeping in a corner of Castle Tioram's courtyard and stole away to sail across to South Uist, he found it awaiting him on the shore, at Lochboisdale. He tried locking it in one of the cells of the castle and sailed off to Arisaig, only to discover the creature swimming alongside his galley. He sought to ignore it, but near the Isle of Eigg a great storm blew up and threatened to sink the ship. In desperation the crewmen pleaded with their Chief to take the thing aboard before they were all drowned, or they would down oars. Eventually the alarmed John agreed, and the storm sank away promptly.

It would be nice to record that this unpleasant creature came to a suitably sticky end; but he in fact died in his bed on the Isle of Canna, in 1686. However his passing was accompanied by signs that perhaps judgement awaited him elsewhere. In the night a piercing whistling was heard, whether from the attendant frog or otherwise is not clear. But it was enough to cause the dying Chief to try to flee his bed. Again and again the dire whistling resounded, and hands to his ears John of Clanranald managed to arise and stagger outside. But he was brought back by his followers, who had to tie him down on the bed. At last, a different sound challenged the whistling, the dawn heralded by a cock crowing thrice — a nice touch that — and Clanranald's desperate spirit moved on to meet his Maker, and perhaps some of his victims.

His son, the thirteenth Chief, was a very different type. Alan Dearg adhered to the Jacobite cause, and in 1715 left Castle Tioram for the last time. Presumably he knew this in some typically Highland way, and as he departed for the wars ordered the place to be set on fire, for he would never return and it must not fall into government hands. He is reported to have turned on a nearby hilltop and watched it burn, sadly, before going on his way. He was killed on the fatal field of Sheriffmuir. Since when Castle Tioram has remained a roofless shell.

Whittinghame Tower
and the Plotters

S et picturesquely among the Lammermuir foothills
three miles south of East Linton, this modest-sized
tower is now the home of the Earl of Balfour. But
originally it was a stronghold of a branch of the great
family of Douglas, who were so strong in East Lothian.
And any Douglas castle was apt to be involved in excitements sooner or later.

Whlttinghame's most significant occasion, surely, was
when in 1567, its laird, Archibald Douglas, a near kinsman of the Earl of Morton, here entertained his Chief,
with the Earl of Bothwell, later the Queen's third husband, and Maitland of Lethington, the Queen's Secretary.
These had some very secret business to transact, and this
remote hold was a suitable place to do it. However, they
did not hold their conference in the tower itself but elected
to do it under the cover of a great and ancient yew-tree
in the garden, even then reputed to be over 300 years old.
The tree's lower branches, as sometimes happens with
yews, had curved over and down and rooted themselves again in the soil, thus creating a dark and hidden
leafy cavern where conspirators could be sure of being
entirely private, with no fears of being overheard. It must
be remembered that many of these old Scots fortalices
were provided with what was known as a laird's lug,
that is a listening device contrived by means of hidden
apertures and shafts in the thickness of the walling, often

alongside the flues of chimneys, whereby conversations held apparently in private could be listened-in to from wall-chambers elsewhere. And on this occasion it was highly important that these plotters should not be overheard; for they were planning the murder of the King.

The King, in this instance, was Henry Stewart, Lord Darnley, who after his marriage to Mary Queen of Scots was granted the Crown Matrimonial. He was, of course, a weakling, but arrogant and very unpopular, and the spirited young queen had quickly tired of him. Bothwell seems to have been the prime mover in this plot, although Lethington and Douglas were entirely in favour — as, later, proved to be many other prominent characters near the throne. But Morton, newly returned from England where he had been in exile after the murder before her eyes of Mary's private secretary, Rizzio, in which he was implicated, was on this occasion cautious. He declared that he was 'unwilling to meddle with new troubles when he had scarcely got rid of an old offence.' Bothwell asserted that he need have no fear, and that it was all at the Queen's desire. Morton answered, 'Bring me then the Queen's handwrit for a

warrant, and you shall have your answer.'

At this the conference was adjourned and Douglas, with Bothwell and Lethington, went to Edinburgh to the Queen. Just what happened then has been debated and disputed ever since; did Mary agree to the murder or did she not? Lethington it was who, having seen the Queen, gave Douglas his message, which was to tell the Earl of Morton that 'the Queen would receive no speech of the matter appointed unto him.' Admittedly this was a some-what vague message, and Douglas said so; but Lethington and Bothwell replied that Morton would have no difficulty in comprehending it. Clearly at least, the plotters were to get no written warrant to proceed. Nevertheless, they went ahead.

We know now that the arrangements concocted at Whittinghame were for Darnley to be murdered at Kirk o' Field, in Edinburgh, one of the most mysterious events in Scottish history, when the house in which he slept, and in which the Queen had just visited him, was blown up with gunpowder, but Darnley's body was found, not slain by the explosion but strangled, as had been his page.

The exact truth of this terrible act will probably never be known, until perhaps the Day of Judgement. Whether Mary had in fact any prior knowledge of it all, I for one would certainly not like to assert. The fact that Mary, with Bothwell, went to Seton Palace and amused herself at archery competitions, the day after Darnley's funeral, is often quoted as indication that she was far from innocent of her husband's death; but it could equally be argued that it only showed, what everyone knew anyway, that she had lost all affection for him. Nevertheless, it was injudicious, to say the least. But then Mary, for all her courage, spirit and beauty, was often injudicious.

It is noteworthy that Whittinghame came into the news only 18 months later, when Mary's half-brother, the Earl of Moray, later Regent, who had been in France, came back to Scotland and was received here at

Whittinghame by the same Morton and Lethington —
although Bothwell was now a fugitive and outlaw. It is
reported that when Moray expressed his horror at the
crime of murdering Darnley, Morton and Lethington cor-
dially sympathised and agreed.

It is perhaps suitable to note that five years later
Lethington died in prison, as a captive of the Earl of
Morton — reported that he had swallowed poison, but
self-administered or not, who knows? And Morton him-
self had his ruthless head chopped off after 1581 by 'the
Maiden'.